Crisis in America:
A Christian Response
By
Garland R. Hunt, Esq.

Praise for *Crisis in America: A Christian Response*

The Word of God says that God will shake the nations so that the nations will come to know Him (Haggai 2:6-8). In a season of national and even global upheaval, my friend Garland R. Hunt brings a timely message in his new book, as he issues a call for the Church to intently seek God's face and take a stand for justice in our generation.

Crisis in America: A Christian Response doesn't shrink back from conflict; rather, it projects a voice of wisdom and clarity into the cultural landscape and offers a better way by which we can pursue lasting peace and unity in our homeland. Garland's experience and faith both speak into the tough issues that have affected many communities across America, and he highlights the steps that we can take to apply the Word of God to moments of racial and cultural turmoil. His emphasis on the believer's identity in Christ provides an edifying lens allowing us to see the actions of others and to act in response with a biblically sound worldview.

Dr. Ché Ahn,
Founder and President, Harvest International Ministry;
Founding and Senior Pastor, Harvest Rock Church, Pasadena, CA;
International Chancellor, Wagner University;
Founder, Ché Ahn Ministries

***

The book, *Crisis in America, A Christian Response*, by Bishop Garland Hunt, is something every Christian and non-Christian should read. The book dives into the hearts and souls of Americans today who are trying to make the puzzle pieces fit and understand how God is working to help us see the solutions He has given us. This is a must-read!

Ken Barun,
Executive Vice President, Billy Graham Evangelistic Association

***

Crisis in America: A Christian Response. As the title indicates, Garland Hunt breaks down the components and causes of the crisis in America that everyone is currently experiencing. What makes this book unique and timely is that he also provides a practical guide for what needs to be done and how we as Christians can apply a biblical worldview to these complex issues. What do these challenges mean from a prophetic point of view? Garland does a great job of outlining what THE WORD says on that point also. Additionally, this book tells Garland's personal story of how and why he changed from a radical activist to a Christian Bishop with a passion for true justice as found in the heart of Christ. You should not miss this book as a Christian and an American.

William G. Boykin,
LTG(R) US. ARMY

***

I have known Garland Hunt for over 30 years. He is a rare asset to the body of Christ - a lawyer, a theologian, and a social activist. The book gives a thoughtful guide for how America can reclaim her heart, her soul, her prophetic destiny, and the blessing of God.

It answers the question of Micah 6:8: "and what doth the LORD require of thee, but to do justly, and to love mercy, and to walk humbly with thy God?" The research is phenomenal and insightful. This is a must-read for Christians entering "A Brave New World" with blurred boundaries.

Harry Jackson,
Senior Pastor of Hope Christian Church;
Founder and Chairman of the High Impact Leadership Coalition;
Co-Author of High Impact African American Churches

***

Garland Hunt is among those voices we most need to hear right now. This is more than a book. It's a treatise on faith and following Jesus in this cultural movement, and it tackles head-on that which would most divide us.

John Stonestreet,
President of Colson Center

Crisis in America: A Christian Response

***

Crisis in America: A Christian Response is long overdue, while simultaneously just in time. It is long overdue because it's about time for a man of God like Bishop Garland Hunt to succinctly address the sign of the times from a biblical worldview. Not that no one else has, but no one else has in the context of these chapters. The book is just in time because it courageously captures the moment of the global COVID-19 pandemic as an undeniably divine indicator that God is calling humanity into account and capturing the attention, first of the body of Christ and its global leadership, and secondly the world to "be still and know that I am God."

Crisis in America: A Christian Response, will inform readers of the times and help us to understand what we should do. It reminds us that Satan is our adversary. He uses familiar systems of politics, economics, injustice, racism, and denominations to keep us at war with one another. He knows and fears the power we possess in unity. Finally, the book calls us to self-examination and repentance and challenges us to seek God's face in casting off all weights that have divided the church and being the unified Body that Christ prayed that we would be. I pray that Crisis in America: A Christian Response will start a fire that evolves into a conflagration that spreads from sea to shining sea.

Dr. Kelvin J. Cochran,
Author of *Who Told You That You Were Naked?*
Chief Operating Officer, Elizabeth Baptist Church, Atlanta, GA

***

Crisis in America: A Christian Response, is a very timely guide on how faith can bring society through some of its most complex and toughest challenges. Bishop Hunt has examined the scripture in this book to provide us with clarity at a time when we need it most.

Kay C. James,
President of The Heritage Foundation;
Former Director of US Personnel Management

***

I am very impressed by his new book. I think he powerfully addresses some of the important issues of our times, and gives sound, biblical wisdom for understanding them, and overcoming them. Very well done.

Rick Joyner,
Founder and Executive Director of MorningStar Ministries

***

Bishop Hunt gets to the heart of the matter in Crisis in America: A Christian Response. Christlike motives are the much needed healing balm for our nation. Evangelist Alveda C. King, Civil Rights for the Unborn.

Alveda King,
Daughter of late slain civil rights activist Rev. A. D. King
and his wife Naomi Barber King;
Director of African American Outreach for Gospel of Life;
Consultant to Africa Humanitarian Christian Fellowship

***

America confronts unprecedented crises: attacks on faith, family break-up and moral decline, racial tension, and the recent COVID-19 pandemic. *Crisis in America: A Christian Response* by my friend Garland Hunt is a timely narrative that will show believers how to be mature in their walk with Christ and be effective ambassadors for Him. Bishop Hunt gives the reader a gimlet-eyed analysis of our challenging times illuminated by his rare spiritual, political, and cultural insight. Most of all, Hunt offers hope for how Christians empowered by the Holy Spirit and equipped with faith can resist evil, serve others, and advance the common good.

Ralph Reed,
Founder and Chairman, Faith & Freedom Coalition

***

Garland Hunt has accomplished the near impossible. He takes the reader on a journey that is uncomfortable and comforting at the same time. We need divine healers in race relations and Garland is one man that can say "rise up and walk."

Lance Wallnau,

President of Lance Learning Group;
International Speaker and Consultant; Author of *God's Chaos Candidate: Donald J. Trump and the American Unraveling*

***

Bishop Garland Hunt is one of my dearest friends and is one of the most accomplished leaders I know around the world. His new book *"Crisis in America"* is a faith-filled prophetic answer with practical solutions for most of the pressing issues of our time! From a law degree from Howard University to an attorney for the U.S. Court of Appeals, to outstanding church planter and leader in many government roles including Commissioner of the Georgia Department of Juvenile Justice and President of Prison Fellowship, he is extremely qualified to speak as a major prophet for our national healing, advancement and spiritual awakening! I highly recommend his new book!

Bob Weiner,
President, Weiner Ministries International

Crisis in America: A Christian Response
By Garland R. Hunt, Esq.

Published by
Advocate Publishing LLC
3245 Peachtree Parkway Ste D #226
Suwanee, GA 30024

ISBN - Hardback: 9781735765204
ISBN – Paper: 9781735765211
eBook ISBN: 97817357652228

First edition: 2020

Printed in the United States of America

Table of Contents

Crisis in America:
A Christian Response
By

Garland R. Hunt, Esq.

Acknowledgements

I like to acknowledge those that were critical in the publishing of this book, *Crisis in America.*

Malaka Grant transcribed many of my messages that became the initial spiritual foundation for the book.

Adneatria (Nita) Brown did the lion's share of the initial draft with hours of discussion, meetings, viewing sermons, talks, and personal impartation

Annika Murray was my advocate and assistant in the attempt of my publishing and marketing the first draft of the book.

Reese Phillips brought it across the finish line. She laboriously oversaw all the editing, design, formatting, and even now is still working to make this book a success.

I thank Bishop Wellington Boone for his spiritual inspiration and encouragement.

I thank Elder Percy Moore for his initial financial support and the late Bobby Jean Moore for their years of encouragement.

Most importantly, I thank my family, my three adult children, Garland Jr, Christa, Jeremy, and their lifetime encouragement to their dad.

And, of course, my wife, Eileen, has always stood by me through all the peaks, valleys, and challenges of making this book a reality. I love my family.

Garland R. Hunt

Foreword

By Bishop Wellington Boone

When I first met Garland Hunt, he was working as a law clerk for the United States Court of Appeals for the Fourth Circuit. He had a passion to be an attorney but he was an attorney for God. His goal was in the field of law, not knowing that the Law of God would be where his heart really was. He possessed wisdom beyond his years and was very mature and developed in his thinking.

Since that time, Garland has worked consistently to correct some things that are wrong in America while encouraging Black Americans to avoid the development of a victim's mentality. As a part of our New Generation Campus Ministries, he came up with the mantra, "The leaders of tomorrow are the followers of Jesus Christ today."

He still believes this, wanting the race of Black people to understand their creative goal, but not to be need-based in their mentality, to understand that they can get anywhere God has assigned them to go. That if Whites are not going to be the example, the Black race should take that mantle, following the Scripture that says "not many wise are called, not many noble, but God has chosen the base things of the world to confound the wise . . . yea, and things which are not, to bring to nought things that are."

His message is that the Bible is a principled book, that heaven and earth shall pass away, but the Word of God endures forever. That's how he lived it. He lives based on the principles of Scripture and then he argues from the Bible to the culture, with the idea of being seated with Christ in heavenly places. The idea that in the beginning was the Word and the Word was with God, and the Word was God. He knows that we are to have a biblical view of life, which is said to be a biblical worldview, not just a human view of life. He admonishes us to not have an earthly view of the Bible, but a biblical view of the earth. He understands that the starting point for discussion and arguing the culture is what the Bible says, not what the culture is saying. And that when there are conflicts in the earth, which there are, that they have to be resolved by Almighty God and the principles of the Bible.

Second Corinthians 5:17 says, "If any man be in Christ, he's a new creation." Garland knows that there are two important things in the new creation story. One, the word of reconciliation, which is something to say. Two, the ministry of reconciliation, which is something to do. And he is clear that first man must be reconciled first back to God. Then the division that started with Adam's transgression in the garden must be applied to the home, that there should be unity in the family, between the husband and the wife. He knows that God hates divorce and it never was a consideration with him, and beyond that, the children got a chance to see unity in the home.

From that, he teaches with clarity and with simplicity. Even though he is an attorney accustomed to doing research and going into primary sources, he doesn't use the grandiloquent words he understands. He doesn't try to use flowery language. He takes complex premises and thoughts and teaches them with simplicity, but yet with a depth of meaning.

Garland Hunt is an amazing man. His message is in demand. He recognizes that the means for accomplishing what the culture will become will come out of the character of a man, and it will be exemplified in the church. The church is to display the reality of God. That's why he understands that judgment first begins with the house of God. The fivefold ministry—apostles, prophets, pastors, teachers, evangelists—are to perfect the saints for the work of the ministry, and through their rebirth and their development the world can see what the church culture is like as an example, and therefore want to become like that.

The light that shines in the darkness—the church, the salt of the earth. The vision of God would be put out by the church. As Proverbs declares, where there is no vision, the people perish. And so the vision of the church will be the inspiration for people to live. Garland is full of vision because he knows that vision is the way that God will get out the truth.

He is bold because timidity—fear—is not authored by God. As Paul told Timothy, God has not given you the spirit of fear, but power and love and a sound mind. The Word says the righteous are bold as a lion. So Garland is bold because he knows that boldness was a primary premise. In Revelation 21 it says the unbelieving and the fearful will find themselves in the Lake of Fire, so he has it as a goal not to be afraid. He knows that to be the example of the church and to put out the vision he needs the Holy Spirit as a major Helper because he is someone who brings the demonstration of the Holy Spirit in the power of God to the culture.

With that power, he possesses passion. Passion means being like Michael Jordan, who wanted the basketball at the end of the game. It means a crunch-time mentality. That is what you need to get things done for God.

Secondly, passion means having compassion. As Jude says, "And some, having compassion, making a difference." The premise is whom you have compassion for, you have a capacity to help. And this is the heartthrob of this man and then the measure of this man.

So there it is—the man, the message, the means, and the measure to look to the whole world. "This gospel of the kingdom shall be preached," it says in Matthew 24, "as a witness to the whole world, and then shall the end come." The signs at the end are wars, rumors of wars, division among households, inclement weather. All these signs seem to be apparent today, but Garland's book is a solution book that not only shows and identifies the signs but also gives the solutions from a primary level.

He has the thoroughness of his legal background, yet with the spirit of the Creator of the world—to the whole world with the whole truth. He is not compromising when he does his research and talks from his sources about what is going on in our culture today and where things began, whether in this generation or generations earlier. As a master craftsman, he identifies the roots of these problems and brings them out so that not only can there be understanding, but also there can be a process of making a difference with no compromise. He displays what God wants done in what is considered the day of the

Lord. Even though he identifies a crisis, he also makes known the solution, so his measure is to the whole world with the whole truth.

He is living for a well-done. In his mind and this book, you will see that what he wants is that God ultimately would say these words over him and that hopefully, he would say over you, as well, "Well done, thy good and faithful servant."

Pleasing God is this man's heartthrob, and I pray it would become your heartthrob also, in the reading of it.

This book done by a master craftsman should be read from youth up to the clergy and professional people because he seems to leave no rock unturned.

God bless you as you read this book.

Bishop Wellington Boone
Atlanta, Georgia

About The Book

Objectives:

> ➤ To define and shape a biblical worldview for the readers by which they may examine and interpret our national calamities

> ➤ To encourage the church in America to become modern-day "Sons of Issachar" and "Nehemiah's," accurately discerning the signs of the times and rebuilding the walls in their communities—starting with their families

> ➤ To survey current societal challenges and controversies and expose the underlying spiritual and relational issues that need to be resolved

> ➤ To challenge today's Christ-followers to be like the ancient Bereans, studying the Word and analyzing America's self-professed prophets through the lens of Scripture

> ➤ To issue a mandate to our country's Christian leaders to use their spiritual and moral authority to prick the consciences of Christians and non-Christians alike

> ➤ To teach churches how to respond with solutions that help and heal the racial conflicts erupting in our country and the sociological tragedies plaguing our communities

"For He, Himself is our peace and our bond of unity. He...made both groups...into one body and broke down the barrier, the dividing wall [of spiritual antagonism between us]...Instead of continuing with two groups of people separated by centuries of animosity and suspicion, He created a new kind of human being, a fresh start for everybody."

Ephesians 2:14–15 AMP

Chapter One

What Time Is It?

"Then He also said to the multitudes, 'Whenever you see a cloud rising out of the west, immediately you say, "A shower is coming"; and so it is. And when you see the south wind blow, you say, "There will be hot weather;" and there is. Hypocrites! You can discern the face of the sky and of the earth, but how is it you do not discern this time?'" – Luke 12:54–56 (NKJV)

There's a popular joke about five elderly ladies in a car inching down the freeway while other vehicles are whizzing by at break-neck speed. Perched on the side of the highway, waiting to catch speeding drivers, a state police officer saw the car creeping along at 22 miles per hour! He thought, *This puttering driver is just as hazardous on the road as a speedy driver!* So, he turned on his lights and siren, tracked down the car, and pulled the driver over.

Approaching the car, he noticed that there were five elderly ladies—two in the front seat and three in the back with eyes as wide as saucers and shaking as if they had seen ghosts.

The driver, perplexed for having been pulled over, queried, "Officer, I don't understand, I was doing exactly the speed limit! What seems to be the problem?"

"Ma'am," the officer replied, "you weren't speeding, but you should know that driving slower than the speed limit can also be a danger to other drivers."

"Slower than the speed limit? No, sir. I was precisely following the speed limit at 22 miles an hour," the woman proudly replied.

The state police officer, holding back a chuckle, explained to her that "22" was the route number, not the speed limit. A bit embarrassed, the woman grinned and thanked the officer for pointing out her error.

"But before I let you go, ma'am, I have to ask. Is everyone in the car okay? Your passengers seem awfully shaken," the officer said.

"Oh, they'll be just fine, officer. We're almost home now. We just got off Route 119, and we're about to get onto Interstate 95!"

Just like that elderly driver, we can also misread signs! Some signs won't result in disastrous consequences if we misread them, but others—if misunderstood—could be fatal! Now, more than ever, God's people need to understand the times we are living in and accurately understand the signs that the Bible warned us would take place so that we can make the right move at the right time.

While in Washington, D.C., I attended a meeting close to the Capitol building. I had a chance to look at the Capitol building, the Rayburn building, and the offices where the United States Senate and Congress meet. As I looked around, everyone was busily moving about as if everything were normal.

In the midst of that hustle and bustle, I contemplated how the White House—the most defended house in the entire world (supposedly)—could be so easily penetrated. How could one man jump the fence, run across the lawn and get inside the White House? He overcame a Secret Service guard and passed the steps that led to the personal residence of the president of the United States. He was armed with a knife. He could have been draped with bombs. Olympus can fall.

The point I am making is we have a facade of safety. We think that somehow, we are immune from the things that are going on everywhere else; but in reality, we can't even secure the White House. The Lord is our only defense. He's our only hedge of protection.

We never thought there would be such a maliciously planned attack to come against our nation as the one that stunned us on September 11, 2001. The White House was Al' Qaeda's target. However, the plane crashed in Pennsylvania. They also took out part of the Pentagon and both Twin Towers in New York City.

Crisis in America: A Christian Response

You don't think the devil is serious? ISIS, the militant, radicalized faction of Islam (even worse than Al' Qaeda), declared that they are going to fly their flag at the White House. That's a bold statement! But their bold statements have been accompanied by bold actions, for this is the same group that was committing the gruesome crimes and beheadings we've seen on the news.

What about global health crises? What are we going to do about them? The World Health Organization (WHO) lists twenty diseases as pandemic or epidemic. At the time of this writing, the entire world is being affected and even devastated by COVID-19. In the United States alone there have been over two million confirmed cases with over one hundred thousand resulting in death.

This coronavirus was allegedly first identified in China's seafood and poultry market in December 2019. Other sources, however, purport that the virus was created in a Wuhan, China lab as a means of biological warfare. Whatever its origin, the coronavirus has spread rapidly and caused unprecedented heightened responses, impacting lives across the globe and forcing everyone into a new normal.

Following guidelines issued by the Center for Disease Control (CDC), schools canceled classes, shopping malls closed, and travel came to an abrupt halt. Churches nationwide resorted to online services only, relying on the use of technology to share the gospel and disciple and train their members.

At the recommendation of the CDC to abandon large gatherings and unnecessary contact, state and local governments issued shelter in place orders, admonishing people to leave their homes only for groceries or essential business. The uncertainty of this disease, the threat of a second wave, and its ability to be transmitted by people who appear to be asymptomatic have caused a stifling fear worldwide.

Rampant police violence. Military unrest. Plagues and disease. Natural disasters. Our nation, our world, is at such a critical place right now. However, God has not lost control. "God is our refuge and strength, always ready to help in times of trouble" (Psalm

46:1, NLT). God does have a way of getting our attention. He's getting the attention of sinners and saints.

Tragic news dominates social media and overshadows our personal and professional conversations. What should Christians think about these global disasters, which seem to arise as constantly as waves rush the shores of our beaches? If God has sovereignly placed His people in the various cities, countries, and towns in which we live, how does He want us to respond when these tragedies hit close to home? How should we interpret the activities and calamities of our day?

The Importance of Having a Biblical Worldview

"The children of Issachar…were men that had understanding of the times, to know what Israel ought to do; the heads of them were two hundred; and all their brethren were at their commandment."
– I Chronicles 12:32

Christians can heroically respond to a crisis *if* we understand the times and know what the nation should do as the children of Issachar did—armed with a biblical worldview and Scriptural remedies to solve the world's ailments.

Dr. Del Tackett, former president of the Focus on the Family Institute and creator of the Truth Project, defines worldview as *"the framework from which we view reality and make sense of life and the world."* Chuck Colson explains worldview as *"the sum total of our beliefs about the world."*

It is not only important to take into consideration that all of us have a worldview but Christians also need to have a perspective that is governed and influenced by the truths taught in the Scriptures—that's what is widely known as a "biblical worldview." Tackett emphasizes that *"a biblical worldview is based on the infallible Word of God. When you believe the Bible is entirely true, then you allow it to be the foundation of everything you say and do."*

Dr. also Tackett reported:

"A recent nationwide survey completed by the Barna Research Group determined that only 4 percent of Americans had a 'biblical' worldview. When George Barna, who has researched cultural trends and the Christian Church since 1984, looked at the 'born-again' believers in America, the results were a dismal 9 percent. Barna's survey also connected an individual's worldview with his or her moral beliefs and actions. Barna says, 'Although most people own a Bible and know some of its content, our research found that most Americans have little idea how to integrate core biblical principles to form a unified and meaningful response to the challenges and opportunities of life."

You may wonder why it is important to have a biblical worldview when analyzing the challenges, we face as a nation. How can the Church, as a "city on a hill" and "the salt and light of the earth," respond with ready answers and sound solutions to crisis after crisis? Tackett hit the nail right on the head when he noted this:

"If we don't really believe the truth of God and live it, then our witness will be confusing and misleading. Most of us go through life not recognizing that our personal worldviews have been deeply affected by the world. Through the media and other influences, the secularized American view of history, law, politics, science, God and man affects our thinking more than we realize. We then are taken 'captive through hollow and deceptive philosophy, which depends on human tradition and the basic principles of this world rather than on Christ (Colossians 2:8)."

However, by diligently learning, applying and trusting God's truths in every area of our lives—whether it's watching a movie, communicating with our spouses, raising our children, or working at the office—WE CAN BEGIN TO DEVELOP A DEEP COMPREHENSIVE FAITH THAT WILL STAND AGAINST THE UNRELENTING TIDE OF OUR CULTURE'S NONBIBLICAL IDEAS. If we capture and embrace more of God's worldview and trust it with

*unwavering faith, then we begin to make the right decisions
and form the appropriate responses to questions on abortion,
same-sex marriage, cloning, stem-cell research, and even
media choices. Because, in the end, it is our decisions and
actions that reveal what we really believe." (Emphasis mine)*

Response #1: Observe World Events Through the Lens of Discernment

We, the Church, must discern the times and discern the body
accurately. The *King James Dictionary* defines the word "discern" as
"*to examine, prove, or test; to scrutinize.*" *The International Standard
Bible Encyclopedia* explains it as follows:

"Five Hebrew words are thus translated: *bin, yadha', nakhar,
ra'ah* and *shama'*. It may simply mean *'observe'* (bin), 'I discerned
among the youths' (Proverbs 7:7); or *discriminating knowledge*, 'A
wise man's heart discerneth time and judgment' (Ecclesiastes 8:5,
yadha'); 'He discerned him not, because his hands', etc. (Genesis
27:23, *nakhar*); 'Then shall ye return and discern between the
righteous and the wicked' (Malachi 3:18, *ra'ah*); 'So is my lord the
king to discern good,' etc. (2 Sa 14:17, *shama'*). In the New
Testament, the words *anakrino, diakrino,* and *dokimazo* are thus
translated, expressing close and distinct acquaintance with or a critical
knowledge of things."

Vine's Expository Dictionary of New Testament Words defines
discernment as examination and learning "by discriminating" in order
to "determine or decide." Discernment seeks "to distinguish, or
separate so as to investigate (*krino*) by looking throughout (*ana,
intensive*) objects or particulars" or in legal terms, "to question, to
hold a preliminary judicial examination preceding the trial proper."

When Christians "discern the times," what they're really doing is
observing the events that are taking place around the world, becoming
familiar or distinctly acquainted with current cultural issues,
examining those issues, and then determining the problem/solution
behind those issues.

Biblical discernment requires a knowledge of God's Word and an
understanding of how God sees our world. Romans 12:2 (NIV) states,

"Do not conform to the pattern of this world, but be transformed by the renewing of your mind." The Message Bible puts Romans 12:1–2 this way:

> *"So here's what I want you to do, God helping you: Take your everyday, ordinary life—your sleeping, eating, going-to-work, and walking-around life—and place it before God as an offering. Embracing what God does for you is the best thing you can do for him. Don't become so well-adjusted to your culture that you fit into it without even thinking. Instead, fix your attention on God. You'll be changed from the inside out. Readily recognize what he wants from you, and quickly respond to it. Unlike the culture around you, always dragging you down to its level of immaturity, God brings the best out of you, develops well-formed maturity in you."*

Discernment Versus Deception

It is important to have proper discernment about what God is doing, about what's happening in the nation, and about what's happening in the church—the body of Christ. The Bible says even the elect would be deceived (Mark 12:22). So, understand this: we are vulnerable to deception. The spirit of deception is coming upon us. The enemy, the devil, wants to confuse the Church and have its members waste time fighting each other about denominations, race, gossip, leadership everything. Nobody likes anybody. We spend our time focusing on each other. We don't use the greatest power known to man; Jesus said the gates of hell shall not prevail against the church (Matthew 16:18). We must have an understanding of what is going on.

> *"The Pharisees also with the Sadducees came, and tempting and desired him that he would shew them a sign from heaven. He answered and said unto them, When it is evening ye say, It will be fair weather: for the sky is red. And in the morning, It will be foul weather today: for the sky is red and lowering. Oh ye hypocrites, YE CAN DISCERN THE FACE OF THE*

SKY; BUT YE CANNOT DISCERN THE SIGNS OF THE TIMES?" – *Matthew 16:1–3 (Emphasis mine)*

Do you know how much a meteorologist is paid to scientifically discern what the weather is going to be like? They can figure out the weather, most of the time, but *we can't discern the times that we are living in.*

It states in verse 4, *"A wicked and adulterous generation seeketh after a sign: and there shall no sign be given unto it, but the sign of the prophet Jonas."* Well, you know what that sign was: repent! God is going to bring judgment to Nineveh. Judgment is coming.

We'd better listen to the voice of the prophet. That's going to be our sign. And missing *this* sign will be more costly than the elderly driver who couldn't discern the signs for speed limits from the signs for route numbers!

Scrutiny Begins with the Church

There is a tendency to think that what we are going through as a nation is the result of misguided people with their own agendas who believe that they can do whatever they want. We wait around to see which leader is going to make the biggest mistake.

We blame the political party that is currently in charge. That's really the problem, right? When the Democrats are in charge, the mantra is that we can fix our nation's problems if we get the Republicans in office. When the Republicans are in charge, then the Democrats say, "All we have to do is get those Republicans out of there and get a Democrat in office to fix the problem."

Before we can fix anything, the Lord is saying to the Church, judgment starts in the house of God. We cannot judge the world until we start scrutinizing and discerning ourselves. Many times in prayer, I would pray against the evil and wickedness of this generation, and then the Lord would turn it on me and would have me deal with the evil and wickedness in me.

Every time we point a finger at someone else, we have four other fingers pointed toward ourselves. We have to get ourselves right first. Before we try to get the speck out of somebody's eyes, we must first remove the log in our own eyes (Matthew 7:5). We may self-righteously criticize the mistakes or decisions that government leaders make when we need to address what's going on inside of us and how God sees us.

We must start with ourselves. We can't discern the times correctly unless we "discern the body" or approach our cultural and moral issues with solemn self-inspection, with pure motives and a repentant heart.

According to *Vine's Expository Dictionary of New Testament Words*, when a person "discerns the body," that person is seeking to first "judge" or "try oneself," "discerning" one's condition, and so "judging any evil before the Lord", regarding partaking of the bread and the cup of the Lord's Supper unworthily, by not 'discerning' or discriminating what they represent.

> *"Wherefore whosoever shall eat of this bread, and drink of this cup of the Lord, unworthily, shall be guilty of the body and the blood of the Lord." – 1 Corinthians 11:27*

Do you see how serious the Apostle Paul is about this? He said if we take communion unworthily without discerning our spiritual condition or without judging any evil in our lives before the Lord, we are guilty of the body and the blood of the Lord. We're just as guilty as the ones who put Jesus on the cross.... if we approach the sacrament of the Lord's Supper the wrong way.

> *"But let a man <u>examine himself,</u> and so let him eat of that bread, and drink of that cup. For he that eateth and drinketh unworthily, eateth and drinketh damnation to himself, not discerning the Lord's body. For this cause many are weak and sickly among you, and many sleep. For if we would <u>judge ourselves,</u> we should not be judged. But when we are judged, we are chastened of the Lord, that we should not be condemned with the world." – 1 Corinthians 11:28–32*

The only way we are not going to be condemned with this world that we are calling a wicked and adulterous generation is if we allow the

Lord to chasten us and if we judge ourselves in keeping with 1 Corinthians.

I thank God for giving us space to repent. When we say or do the wrong thing, we can cry out for His blood. We can say, "Thank You, Lord, that You died for me." The Lord knows that we're going to fall below the standard—which is why He died for us. The nasty sins that we commit, the perfect Lamb put them upon Himself so that we can come before Him and confess our sins and ask the Lord to forgive our sins. His blood will cleanse us from all unrighteousness. We must live in a constant state of repentance. The Bible says that he who is without sin is a liar (1 John 1:8).

Maybe we didn't kill anyone. Perhaps we've never committed adultery. However, we can still scrutinize our own lives for faults or secret sins that no one else sees but God. What about our thoughts, our attitudes, and cravings inside of us that are not visible? What are our motivations that no one can see but God? How do we react when people mistreat us? How does it make us feel? We have to deal with the hidden issues of our hearts. We have to deal with the conscious sins as well as the unconscious. We must acknowledge that sin is present in our lives and hearts and we must repent and ask the Lord to help us, to purify us.

The first step to repentance is brokenness. God wants us broken. He opposes pride, but He gives grace to the humble. So, we need grace; we need His mercy. In the midst of great trial and suffering all around us, we need His grace to encompass us. Therefore, we must maintain a posture of brokenness.

Is there ever a time in which we are truly broken before God? At some point, there has to be something—a cry or a prayer. Perhaps on an individual level, there's a time of admitting our vulnerability to God or yielding to a sensitivity to God in which we cry out to Him.

It's hard to be sensitive to God when you're stubborn or resistant to God's holy "nudges," thinking that public displays of prayer, worship, or going to the altar are not for you. However, at some point, there has to be brokenness.

Jesus cried in the Garden of Gethsemane, "let this cup pass from Me!" (Matthew 26:29). He sweated great drops of blood. He knew what was ahead. He thought of His disciples and He prayed for them. He cried out to His Father, "Lord, don't forsake me." Even Jesus showed emotion. He looked at Israel, and He wept. His people didn't discern what was going on. They were seeking the Messiah for what He could do, not who He was. So, if at some point Jesus' heart was broken, are we too good to be broken?

At some point, we have to be broken by something other than ourselves. Is there anything from God that breaks us? Think about His longsuffering. Think about how He keeps us. He loves us so much. How can we be saved and never be broken? There has to be a tender place in our hearts for Him. If we can't have a tender place for Him, how can we have a tender place for a sinner? How can we love someone else without loving God? Jesus wasn't weeping because of Himself. He wept because of their lack of discernment. They didn't see. God is going to deal with us, but His dealings will give us much more power.

Men can be prideful; they want to display their male ego. However, a truly broken man is a powerful man. God most likely programmed men that way for leadership. However, if it is not handled appropriately, leadership can stand against God because we feel like we are out of control if we yield too much. I pray that we never get to a place in which God cannot break us. I pray that brokenness comes by revelation, not by circumstances.

Spiritual Warfare and Prayer

"Finally, my brethren, be strong in the Lord and the power of His might. Put on the whole armor of God, that you may be able to stand against the wiles of the devil. For we do not wrestle against flesh and blood, but against principalities, against powers, against the rulers of the darkness of this age, against spiritual hosts of wickedness in the heavenly places."
– Ephesians 6:10–12 (NKJV)

This country is not fighting a flesh and blood fight. The true fight is not with presidents, legislators, rogue judges, politicians, supervisors, mayors, or governors. Change does not come by replacing the people in these positions. It doesn't matter who the individuals are. If their hearts are not fully committed to God, they are still going to operate in the realm of the flesh.

Somebody has to cry out to God in prayer. However, we cannot sit back and pray without taking action. Christians must get involved in the marketplace. We need to go into the areas in which we are graced by God and represent the Lord as an ambassador. We need to represent the Kingdom of God wherever we are.

God has called us to stand in prayer corporately and individually. We must stand even when no one else is standing. While praying, God will expand your vision. When you're praying in tongues, you don't even know what you are praying. As God prays through you, He will take you to the nations. Your earnest prayers will take you beyond your personal needs and have you praying for others.

We shouldn't let anything keep us from praying. The Lord says, "...the prayer of a righteous man avails much" (James 5:16, NKJV). We may not see the effects or the power of our prayers, but our prayers are availing. We may pray about something for months or even years and not see anything happen. Anna the Prophetess prayed for years for Jesus to come on the scene. She was frail and at the end of her life when He came. We may pray for things we never see, but it is still worth our prayers.

There is spiritual warfare going on because the enemy wants to destroy our faith. He would have us to believe that we won't see the manifestation of our prayers. He doesn't want us to believe that our prayers have power. Nonetheless, God wants us to remain steadfast in our faith, believing for the things we have been praying for. He only responds to faith. He will not respond to our whining, tears, or pity parties. He responds when our faith is where it needs to be. He wants the things we have been praying for: souls for the Kingdom.

Our prayers have incredible power. The Bible says one can put a thousand to flight (Joshua 23:10). What would happen if we all came together in prayer? If you feel weak in your prayer life, get connected to someone with a strong prayer life. Find out what motivates them when they pray. Don't be prideful and miss the power we can have when we pray together.

Ephesians 6:13–18 states:

"Wherefore take onto you the whole armour of God, that ye may be able to withstand in the evil day, having done all, to stand. Stand, therefore, having your loins girt about with truth, and having on the breastplate of righteousness; And your feet shod with the preparation of the gospel of peace; Above all, taking the shield of faith, wherewith ye shall be able to quench all the fiery darts of the wicked. And take the helmet of salvation, the sword of the Spirit, which is the word of God: Praying always with all prayer and supplication in the Spirit, watching thereunto with all perseverance and supplication for all saints...."

Pray always. We can't get any further if we don't recognize that our first call is to pray. We have to seek His face. We can stay out there on the outer court, praying for stuff and never getting there with God.

Some of us have never gotten to the holy of holies, and sometimes, we need to help each other get beyond the veil. This is the beginning of how to respond to what we are dealing with at this time.

Chapter Two

Whom Shall I Fear?

"Jesus replied… 'Those who love their life in this world will lose it. Those who care nothing for their life in this world will keep it for eternity. Anyone who wants to serve me must follow me, because my servants must be where I am. And the Father will honor anyone who serves me.'" – John 12:23, 25–26

Living with a Sensitivity to God's Agenda

Christians must have discernment in this hour. Discernment is sharpened by allowing the Lord to deal with our hearts. If we don't open our hearts, we don't stand a chance in this day. We must be able to discern the body of Christ, the times we live in, and ourselves.

How sensitive are Christians to the spiritual, political, and physical environment of our day? We can be controlled by the media and not realize it. If the media focus is on the elections, we will forget about Ebola. If the news media is focused on ISIS, we will forget about the economy. We have to discern correctly and keep ourselves right before the Lord. We cannot discern outside of ourselves unless we are willing to discern within ourselves.

The church provides a breeding ground for singers and musicians. There are also many popular preachers to whom the world enjoys listening. We like to be entertained in church. We like to erect beautiful, impressive church buildings and temples. However, the Lord's house is not a house of singing, preaching, broadcasting, or constructing buildings. It's a house of prayer.

Is it possible that we are focusing on the wrong things? Is it possible that the things we flock to are not God's priorities at all? He looks for a man who will stand in the gap on behalf of others. When

God judged Sodom and Gomorrah, it wasn't about the number of people in sin. The terms of negotiation between Abraham and God were concerning the number of righteous people there were in Sodom and Gomorrah (Genesis 18:23-33). If the destruction of America were based on the prevalence of prayer, would the Lord bring judgment upon us if a thousand people were praying in this nation? In many cases, we have a misplaced understanding of what is important to God.

David was a man after God's own heart. The Lord directed his son, Solomon, to build a temple. He gave Solomon riches and wisdom. However, Solomon still did not have the heart of his daddy. There was something pure about his daddy's heart. The Lord wants us to keep our hearts pure. The only way to do this is with a consistent relationship with the living God. We need to ask the Lord to help us find that place with Him.

When we come before the Lord, God will begin to deal with us. We cannot find ourselves in a prideful place. The Bible speaks of the wheat and the tares growing together (Matthew 13:24-30). Sometimes, we feel like God is sensitizing us to the things of the Spirit, that we are opening up to the things of God. At the same time, we can be overtaken by natural, everyday situations and the things of life that are trying to entangle us.

The Bible says that a good soldier doesn't ensnare himself with the affairs of this life (1 Timothy 2:3-4). That admonition reveals there is a potential for Christians to be entangled. A good soldier can potentially become entangled when "life comes at us." If we are not aggressive in seeking and prioritizing our relationship with the Lord to overcome the natural, everyday things that try to pull us in, we can become entangled.

Once we begin to make a stand to get it right and surrender to the Lord, the devil often responds with an onslaught of opposition. The enemy wants to see if we really mean what we say. Sickness, disease, and a host of challenges may spring up. This is why prayer is so necessary. Even when we are going through something, we need to pray. Pray for each other without ceasing.

Most of the preaching in the Bible took place outside of the church. The voice of what is preached must go out. The messages we hear in church will manifest fruit in our personal lives if we act on them. Bible teaching encourages us to pray and read the Word of God. It encourages us to get our priorities in order. However, what causes the message to go out is what we speak to others. We cannot hold it to ourselves. There is a passion that we cannot deny.

The Strategy of Our Enemy, the Devil

Be not ignorant of the devil's devices! In the last days, there will be false prophets and apostles. There will be false doctrines coming to the Church in a greater way. It's vital for us to have a strong biblical foundation. We need a daily diet of the Word of God. Start today to prepare for tomorrow.

When the winds and waves of adversity hit, we won't be able to run to the Bible. If we don't possess a treasured knowledge of God's Word in us at that moment, we will be overtaken by whatever is coming against us.

I support education. However, an academic degree will not give us victory in the day of struggle. A relationship with the living God, an understanding of His ways, and a strong biblical foundation will give us victory in the day of struggle.

The enemy will attack us through emotions, circumstances, and situations. He will even come against what we believe. The Bible says even the elect will be deceived (Mark 12:22). The Bible is not just a bunch of fables; it is real.

The devil is called *"the prince of the power of the air"* in Ephesians 2:2, which means he is the commander of certain powers in the unseen world. There will be natural circumstances and a spiritual attack against the Church. Some people will rise up and have a great influence around the world. They will speak of all the things we "need." However, there will be no mention of Jesus or a moral foundation to empower and give meaning to what we do. We will wonder if our foundation is necessary.

However, we must not be deceived; without a vital relationship with Jesus Christ and a strong faith in life beyond this world, we may become prey to fearing death due to the constant threats to our physical safety in these troubled times.

Response #2: Overcome Fear—Particularly the Fear of Death

"God is our shelter and our strength. When troubles seem near, God is nearer, and He's ready to help. So why run and hide? No fear, no pacing, no biting fingernails. When the earth spins out of control, we are sure and fearless. When mountains crumble and the waters run wild, we are sure and fearless. Even in heavy winds and huge waves, or as mountains shake, we are sure and fearless." – Psalm 46:1–3 (VOICE)

The body of Christ must respond to crisis and the rise in worldwide Christian persecution with a determination to "stare down" fear. *"For God did not give us the spirit of fear, but of power and of love and of a sound mind"* (2 Timothy 1:7, NKJV). God is not the author of fear.

We must overcome the fear of death. The Bible states that we die daily (1 Corinthians 15:31). However, there is something about our mortality that keeps us holding onto life. We must understand the world from an eternal viewpoint. Everything we go through has an impact on eternity. Our consciousness has to be eternal. We have to fight for it.

We wrestle with carnal flesh, but the weapons of our warfare are not carnal. It's hard to be rejuvenated when we allow the enemy to take us to a place where we are worn out by our flesh. Let's not get worn out by a lack of spirituality. We have to know where to draw the line.

The Length of Time on Earth Vs the Use of Time on Earth

A godly perspective of our brief assignment on earth might help us overcome the fear of death. Is it the length of time we live on earth or the use of the time we have that really matters? Instead of offering our best investment of time, talents, and treasures on this brief, earthly assignment, we should make our best investments count for eternity.

"In those days Hezekiah became ill and was at the point of death. The prophet Isaiah the son of Amoz went to him and, 'This is what the LORD says: Put your house in order, because you are going to die; you will not recover.' Hezekiah turned his face to the wall and prayed to the LORD...." – 2 Kings 20:1–2 (NIV)

When Hezekiah encountered his crisis, he didn't fuss about the prophecy. He immediately turned to God. When something is going on that we cannot understand or control, we must immediately turn to God. Stop spending so much time with the ones that are bringing stuff to us and spend time with God.

Hezekiah called out to God in prayer: *"'Remember, LORD, how I have walked before you faithfully and with wholehearted devotion and have done what is good in your eyes.' And Hezekiah wept bitterly"* (2 Kings 20:3, NIV).

Can we say that we have walked faithfully before God? Hezekiah had the right to cry out to God because his heart was pure.

"Before Isaiah had left the middle court, the word of the LORD came to him: 'Go back and tell Hezekiah, the ruler of my people, 'This is what the LORD, the God of your father David, says: I have heard your prayer and seen your tears....'" – 2 Kings 20:4–5a (NIV)

Immediately, God heard his prayer. Before Isaiah could get out of the courtyard, God said he would heal him.

"'I will heal you. On the third day from now you will go up to the temple of the LORD. I will add fifteen years to your life. And I will deliver you and this city from the hand of the king of Assyria. I will defend this city for my sake and for the sake of my servant David.'" – 2 Kings 20:5b–6 (NIV)

His righteous walk affected his life and the city he oversaw.

"Then Isaiah said, 'Prepare a poultice of figs.' They did so and applied it to the boil, and he recovered." – 2 Kings 20:7 (NIV)

Until God revealed it, no one knew that the figs were a source of healing. The answer was right there with Him. God can use whatever method for healing that He chooses, i.e., supernaturally, through medication, holistically, etc. Whatever method He uses, it's still His healing, His miracle. However, healing will only take place if, and when God says so.

"Hezekiah had asked Isaiah, 'What will be the sign that the LORD will heal me and that I will go up to the temple of the LORD on the third day from now? Isaiah answered, 'This is the LORD's sign to you that the LORD will do what he has promised: Shall the shadow go forward ten steps, or shall it go back ten steps?'

"'It is a simple matter for the shadow to go forward ten steps,' said Hezekiah. 'Rather, have it go back ten steps.' Then the prophet Isaiah called on the LORD, and the LORD made the shadow go back the ten steps it had gone down on the stairway of Ahaz." – 2 Kings 20:8–11 (NIV)

The sun had to change its position to move back on the dial. God made the time go backward to show them that He was in charge.

"At that time Marduk-Baladan son of Baladan king of Babylon sent Hezekiah letters and a gift, because he had heard of Hezekiah's illness. Hezekiah received the envoys and showed them all that was in his storehouses—the silver, the gold, the spices and the fine olive oil—his armory and everything found among his treasures. There was nothing in his palace or in all his kingdom that Hezekiah did not show them.

"Then Isaiah the prophet went to King Hezekiah and asked, 'What did those men say, and where did they come from?"

"'From a distant land,' Hezekiah replied. 'They came from Babylon.' The prophet asked, 'What did they see in your palace?"'

"'They saw everything in my palace,' Hezekiah said. 'There is nothing among my treasures that I did not show them. 'Then Isaiah said to Hezekiah, 'Hear the word of the LORD: The time will surely come when everything in your palace, and all that your predecessors have stored up until this day, will be carried off to Babylon. Nothing will be left, says the LORD. And some of your descendants, your own flesh and blood who will be born to you, will be taken away, and they will become eunuchs in the palace of the king of Babylon.'"

"'The word of the LORD you have spoken is good,' Hezekiah replied. For he thought, 'Will there not be peace and security in my lifetime?' As for the other events of Hezekiah's reign, all his achievements and how he made the pool and the tunnel by which he brought water into the city, are they not written in the book of the annals of the kings of Judah? Hezekiah rested with his ancestors. And Manasseh his son succeeded him as king." – 2 Kings 20:12–20 (NIV)

It's not *how long* we live; it's *how* we live. Fifteen extra years didn't help Hezekiah. His possessions and inheritance were lost. His offspring were captured and served in the palace of an ungodly king.

What is the purpose of a long life if we are not going to live for the Lord? We cannot control the length of our lives, but we can control the quality of our lives. We must prioritize *eternal life*, not a *long life*.

Why Do Christians Fear Death?

Because we haven't completed our work on the earth, the arrival of death would be premature. However, God is in control of our life on earth and the timing of our death, so we have to use each day wisely. We cannot say we have ten years to accomplish something. We have to live for God now. It's hard to seek God with veracity when we are sick or in pain. Now is the time. We cannot put off giving God a greater level of commitment, dedication, or consecration. We must understand how quickly the bottom can fall out. We cannot put off what God is asking us to do.

If God is saying, "Come," we should come. If He says, "Go," we need to go. If He says, "Seek My face," seek it like never before! If we feel a burden to pray, we must do it right now. We must lay aside our agenda.

Whatever we have to do, we need to do it now. We can't wait on anyone else. We need to seek God for ourselves. We cannot run from terrorism, disease, or natural circumstances. How do you run from an earthquake or flood? We can have the best evacuation plan, but we cannot run when God allows terrible things to happen on this earth. The more we turn away from God, the greater the turmoil will be.

Most people are afraid of death because they are afraid to face God. However, we face God every day. No matter where we are, God is there. We have such an attachment to this life and the things with which we are familiar. However, the Bible tells us, if we love this life, we will lose it (John 12:25).

Our attachment to this life is familiar, but we are unfamiliar with heaven. We wonder if what we've read and heard is real. We would rather stay here with the familiar. However, we can't let the devil deceive us.

Christians are simply pilgrims on earth, ambassadors of the Kingdom. We are just passing through on our way to somewhere else. However, every day counts. When we come before the Lord, we will give an account for every day. Every word that we have spoken will either bless or condemn us. We have to cut our love for this life. We love life based on the stewardship God has assigned us. However, we should desire to be with the Lord more than being here.

Sometimes, we fear death because we fear the agony and pain that can be associated with death. We fear *how* we will die. We don't want to experience an agonizing death. God can take us out instantly.

Why Doesn't Radical Islam Fear Death?

Muslims are convinced that the afterlife is greater than their present life. Part of their teaching is that they are going to paradise. The greatest goal for them is to die as a martyr and receive their special reward. Therefore, they are willing to wrap themselves with suicide bombs. We call it radical Islam.

How can someone in a cult, being deceived, going straight to hell, serving another god, accursed because of Abraham's flesh, still multiply and prosper? It is because they are Abraham's seed.

Where are the radical Christians?

Be Willing to Abandon Life on Earth for the Cause of Christ

As Christians, we must be willing to die for our faith. We must die to public opinion and to the knowledge of what others think of us. We must be willing to die if everyone turns against us. We must be willing to die the ultimate death. We hold onto this world because we don't have a true revelation of eternity. If we did, we would be longing for it.

Death is not a punishment; eternal death and damnation are punishment. Death is the door to the eternal—a good or bad eternity. Let's not die because of our flesh but rather be martyrs for God.

Chapter Three

What Then Shall We Say?

There is victory in death.

"So when this corruptible shall have put on incorruption, and this mortal shall have put on immortality, then shall be brought to pass the saying that is written, Death is swallowed up in victory. O death, where is thy sting? O grave, where is thy victory? The sting of death is sin; and the strength of sin is the law. But thanks be to God, which giveth us the victory through our Lord Jesus Christ. Therefore, my beloved brethren, be ye steadfast, unmoveable, always abounding in the work of the Lord, forasmuch as ye know that your labour is not in vain in the Lord." – I Corinthians 15:54–58

We discovered in the last chapter that death is not the ultimate negative; it is the door that opens eternity. That is why the apostles were able to live on this earth and sustain the suffering they went through. Death is swallowed up in victory.

We have been equipped with a biblical worldview by which we can examine and interpret mankind's activities on the earth. With this God-centered mindset, the first response that Christians should have to a crisis is to discern "the signs of the times" and discern ourselves.

The Church of Jesus Christ is called to courageously rise up and take her place in the battle against the devil's onslaughts in the earth. To do this, Christians must not fear death—our second response to a crisis—but endeavor to make an eternal mark on our generation by sacrificing our lives to win souls for the Kingdom.

Response #3: Deploy God's Five-fold Ministry to His Church

The third response that Christians should have to a crisis is to deploy the five-fold ministry to the Church and the world. In so doing, Christians will be releasing a prophetic voice to the nation and the Church during a critical time in history.

What is the Five-fold Ministry?

In Ephesians 4:11–13, it states this:

> *"And He Himself gave some to be apostles, some prophets, some evangelists, and some pastors and teachers, for the equipping of the saints for the work of the ministry, for the edifying of the body of Christ, till we all come to the unity of the faith and of the knowledge of the Son of God, to a perfect man, to the measure of the stature of the fullness of Christ...."*

The Bible teaches that when the resurrected Christ Jesus ascended into heaven, He handed out ministry "gifts" to His Church to train His followers in skilled service for His Kingdom and to help them fully develop and mature into His likeness.

Those five areas of ministry are the following:

1. Apostles who lay the foundation on which others can build ministries. The apostolic ministry plants churches and encourages the leaders of those churches.

2. Teachers who instruct in the Word of God

3. Pastors who shepherd God's flock and care for their souls

4. Evangelists who have a passion for spreading the Word of God to the people, preaching the Gospel. They understand that the Gospel message and the cross must be preached.

5. Prophets who have the role of foretelling and understanding the times.

God Desires to Use His Prophetic Voice in the Earth

The prophetic can push Christians toward their calling. The prophetic can be a call to the nations and tell others what the Lord wants to say to mankind. The church needs someone who can speak on behalf of God.

All of this is for "the perfecting of the saints," for the work of the ministry, and the edifying of the body of Christ. King David needed Nathan the prophet to come to him. He had committed murder and adultery. Nathan had to bring him the word of the Lord.

It has been a long time since we have seen the combination of the king and the prophet walking together. Even though we are in the New Testament era, there is still an important need for the voice of God. We the church should represent the voice of God.

However, we are divided. Some churches condone same-sex marriages. Some churches say it's okay to turn a blind eye on the things that are not pleasing to God, especially if you have a talent that you are using for the Church. It is difficult to have a righteous standard if you are not living a righteous standard. Because of that, the prophetic voice from the church is significantly weakened. Therefore, our national leadership does not have a prophetic voice speaking to it.

The Word of God Addresses Society's Errors

"Then the word of the LORD came unto me, saying, Before I formed thee in the belly I knew thee; and before thou camest forth out of the womb I sanctified thee, and I ordained thee a prophet unto the nations." – Jeremiah 1:4–5

That Scripture alone should deal with anyone who has questions about how God feels about abortion. How is it that God chose to house a child in the womb, but the womb ends up being the most dangerous place for a child to live?

In our society, as long as the baby is in the womb, it can be a target for murder. However, one day later, after the baby leaves the womb, you will be charged with murder if you kill it. Life is present at conception, but we have decided that if the baby is still in the womb, we can murder it. God is not okay with that.

Our concern about pro-life is not a political position. The Scripture is clear. The circumstances present at the moment of conception do not negate God's Word.

Consider these startling statistics:

- In New York City, for every 1,000 black babies born alive, 1,489 are aborted.
- 73% of abortions in Georgia are on African-American and Latino women.
- 79% of Planned Parenthood facilities are within a two-mile walking radius of the African-American and Latino neighborhoods. This is by design.

The History of Margaret Sanger and Planned Parenthood

Margaret Sanger, the founder of Planned Parenthood, launched the Negro Project in which black pastors were paid to teach and preach birth control. Sanger felt that the Negro race should not be reproduced. In his book, *Black Self-Genocide: What Black Lives Matter Won't Say*, Bishop Wellington Boone notes:

"In 1932, The Birth Control Review, a magazine that she had founded but had since left to her successors to edit, devoted an entire issue to the "Negro Problem.""

"Sanger wanted Black women and other poor women of lower races to have fewer babies because she was a eugenicist who believed in fit and unfit races, and Blacks were not members of her favored race."

"Sanger wrote prolifically and spoke with great clarity about her passion for decreasing the birth rate of people she considered unfit because they were poor, involved in crime, or apparently incapable of being educated."

"Even well-known Black leaders like W.E.B, DuBois, a charter member of the NAACP, wrote articles to exhort Blacks to reduce their population."

"Other prominent pastors and doctors added their voices to the message."

"What began as birth control has become the holocaust of abortion. What began a genocide has become self-genocide. Through the liberalization of abortion laws in Roe v. Wade, Black women were released to kill their own race through abortion.

"Through birth control and abortions, Planned Parenthood, the organization she founded, continues to devalue unborn Black babies as non-persons, just as the U.S. Constitution and the Confederate Constitution describes slaves."

Aborting the Prophetic Voice

There is a natural abortion and a spiritual abortion. Spiritual abortion takes place when we don't fulfill our call when we let other things come into our lives that keep us from doing what God has called us to do. If the enemy cannot kill us in the womb, he will do anything he can to keep us from fulfilling what God has called us to do. We don't have the five-fold ministry or the prophetic operating as it should because we have many excuses.

However, we are not too young; we don't lack the right words because the Lord is going to put the words in our mouths. Whatever God has called us to do, He is going to prepare us to do. We cannot let the devil keep us from doing what we know to do, no matter what the call of God is on our lives.

God has a prophetic voice. It deals with us first, as He dealt with the biblical prophets: Zechariah, Samuel, Nathan, Elijah, Elisha, Jonah, Micah, Joel, Amos, Hosea, Isaiah, Zephaniah, Daniel, Ezekiel, Jeremiah, Haggai, and Malachi. They dealt with the children of Israel first. They dealt with what we would today call the Church.

God told Jeremiah that He was going to do some things, and after He dealt with that, God told him: "See, I have this day set thee over the nations and over the kingdoms, to root out, and to pull down, and to destroy, and to throw down, to build, and to plant" (Jeremiah 1:10).

This is what we are missing. Without a prophetic voice in our nation, horrible things are happening. We are trying to build on a false foundation. The prophetic will come in and root things out. The prophetic voice will soften the ground. No one can stand in the face of God and not break. When we come before God and know it's God, we will fall to the ground no matter who we think we are.

Ezekiel 2:1–4 states this:

> *"And he said unto me, Son of man, stand upon thy feet, and I will speak unto thee. And the spirit entered into me when he spake unto me, and set me upon my feet, that I heard him that spake unto me. And he said unto me, Son of man, I send thee to the children of Israel, to a rebellious nation that hath rebelled against me: they and their fathers have transgressed against me, even unto this very day. For they are impudent children and stiffhearted. I do send thee unto them; and thou shalt say unto them, Thus saith the Lord GOD."*

Don't be moved by what you see. Sometimes, God is giving us a prophetic word for someone around us, and we should expect that word to come forth. We don't have to be religious. Just speak naturally and share what the Lord said. God will back us up; He will validate the word. Individually, we have a prophetic word in us. However, some have a tremendous gifting or calling for the prophetic.

The prophetic is not for entertainment. We have used the gift in the church to get the attention of the congregation or to renew our faith. But that is just the beginning of it. God wants the prophetic word to go forth to speak His truth. It will shock not only the church but also the world.

There is an absence of the prophetic in the nation. No matter the circumstance, God is the one with the power to make this nation work. We should never get confident in man's ability to fix things. We must have a prophetic voice that will speak in our nation and among us.

The devil has been keeping us distracted by our personal circumstances, and God has not been able to get to our hearts. However, God wants to use us to impact the lives of others. They are waiting for us. They need us in communities and schools. Unimaginable death, destruction, and grievous things are happening that never would have happened twenty years ago. The devil is saying, "Unless the Church rises up, I'm going to have my way."

The Church is a sleeping giant. We are the ones whom God called. We can stand our ground. Therefore, we cannot be afraid of God using us. If He cannot use us one-on-one, He sure cannot use us to shock a nation corporately.

Right now, He is pulling forth the prophetic out of us. There is a lot of "Jeremiah" or "Nathan" inside of us. We need to thank God that we were not killed before we were born. How many "Jeremiahs" have been killed before they were allowed to come out of the womb?

God allows us free will, but He is not happy with us as a nation. There has to be a stirring inside of us that says, "It has to stop." The political pundits are being heard. Where are the righteous men and women of God? Someone has to point the finger and say, "If you don't change, whoever you are, God's judgment is coming."

There has to be a stirring inside of us that declares, "Enough is enough!" We are allowing TV programs to deceive us. Shonda Rhimes was given an award for using her TV shows to elevate the gay agenda and other perversions so that it appears normal, tolerated, or easier to accept.

At some point, a prophet has to come forth. Are we strong enough to go against our own families because they love the entertaining storylines so much? Will there be consequences if we criticize the actions of highly regarded black celebrities? It's about God or ungodliness, righteousness, or unrighteousness. It has nothing to do with race.

Will people get angry at us? Of course, they will. They will call us names and accuse black Christians of forgetting the sacrifices of those who have gone before them, but Christians have to stand for righteousness. We don't want to be on the wrong side of God. We have to draw the line in the sand like the biblical prophets.

One of the kings of Israel was surrounded by prophets who were paid to tell him what he wanted to hear. But Micah proclaimed that he would only speak what God says (Micah 3:5-8). We have to stand for truth. We cannot identify with the masses. We must love people enough to tell them the truth. Our voices must proclaim the truth to the generations. There has to be a prophetic call that comes out of the church.

As African Americans, we should voluntarily walk in humility. Instead, the enemy stirs up pride in us. There has to be a prophetic call that comes out of the church. The five-fold ministry is for the perfecting of the saints. But first, we have to invite the Lord in to deal with us.

We cannot speak of Jeremiah unless we talk about how God ordained him from the womb. God ordained us before our mothers even saw us. God ordained us as prophets to the nations. If there are things that need to be set right, get it right, for God is beckoning us to the next level.

Chapter Four

Is This Post Taken?

The World is in Crisis

We are living in serious times, and the Lord is pushing us somewhere. He wants us to find a place in Him in which we not only survive but also take ground.

The crises that we have been dealing with lately are real. We cannot avoid or overlook them. As the world becomes interdependent on each other, our communication gets closer. If anything happens in the world, we can get the information instantly. There is no safe place.

We cannot be casual Christians because the world is looking for us to demonstrate who Christ is, what He is saying, and what He would do in the midst of crisis.

The heavens are not in crisis. God knows exactly what is going on. He preordained that we would be alive at this time. Therefore, He is expecting something from us. We are not just here by chance. We cannot sit back and watch these situations as they evolve. We must be involved.

Suicide bombers are deceived into thinking they will earn a place in paradise for strapping a bomb to themselves and killing as many people as possible, including martyring themselves. If people can be deceived to that level of deception, why would we allow the enemy to make us back down?

The youth are the future of this generation. They cannot hide behind their age. God has ordained them for this moment. They carry revival inside of them. Therefore, we should prepare them and challenge them. We need to hear of revival breaking out in our youth.

If a sixteen-year-old has no excuse, how can a sixty-year-old have one? We cannot play around. We must act upon what we hear God say. We cannot leave the church services and not address what we heard.

Response #4: Occupy Our Post as an Intercessor and Watchman

The fourth response that Christians must have to a crisis is to occupy our post as an intercessor and a watchman. When we feel like we are all right with God, usually we are not. There are still things that we need to work out. Before we can pray for a nation, we must find out where we are ourselves.

Proverbs 8:33–35 states, *"Hear instruction, and be wise, and refuse it not. Blessed is the man that heareth me, watching daily at my gates, waiting at the posts of my doors. For whoso findeth me findeth life, and shall obtain favour of the LORD."*

The Lord's Door: Prayer

The first post is the Lord's door. We must seek God first. We must seek Him daily. We cannot be watchmen without seeking His face. We must look for Him.

He wants to give us more of Him than we have. We struggle to spend time with God because we are not spending time with Him regularly. We need to start where we are and increase our time with God. When God beckons us, we need to make time. He wants us desperately.

There are no excuses for not having an active prayer life. When we find Him, we find life. At some point, what we pray in secret will manifest in the public.

We are in training for what God has called us to do. God prepared David to fight the Philistines by having him kill bears that were threatening the sheep. We cannot waste time by being idle.

"Finally, my brethren, be strong in the Lord, and in the power of his might. Put on the whole armour of God, that ye may be able to stand against the wiles of the devil. For we wrestle not against flesh and blood, but against principalities, against powers, against the rulers of the

darkness of this world, against spiritual wickedness in high places. Wherefore take unto you the whole armour of God, that ye may be able to withstand in the evil day, and having done all, to stand. Stand therefore, having your loins girt about with truth, and having on the breastplate of righteousness; And your feet shod with the preparation of the gospel of peace; Above all, taking the shield of faith, wherewith ye shall be able to quench all the fiery darts of the wicked. And take the helmet of salvation, and the sword of the Spirit, which is the word of God: Praying always with all prayer and supplication in the Spirit, and watching thereunto with all perseverance and supplication for all saints; And for me, that utterance may be given unto me, that I may open my mouth boldly, to make known the mystery of the gospel, For which I am an ambassador in bonds: that therein I may speak boldly, as I ought to speak." – Ephesians 6:10–20

Before we stand on our post, we must put on our armor. We need protection, for the enemy wants to destroy us. God wants us to be aware of the strategies of the enemy.

The enemy will use whatever or whomever he can. It doesn't matter who we are or how long we have been saved. The enemy comes against us through other people. The Bible identifies the devil's activity as "the spirit at work in the hearts of those who refuse to obey God" (Ephesians 2:2, NLT).

Our armor helps us to defeat the enemy. We should spend more time fighting in the spiritual realm than wrestling against flesh and blood. We must prepare ourselves for spiritual warfare.

God knows every situation we face. He is our only option. Therefore, we should surrender ourselves to God. We must gird ourselves with God's truth.

It's hard to have confidence in God if things are not right in our lives. Our lifestyles impact our hearts. We need our armor on in our prayer life. We cannot cast down anything if our hearts are not pure. The prayers of the righteous avail much.

We need to pray for each other. We need to pray for the saints. We must pray for our leaders. When God lays someone on our hearts, we need to respond.

The enemy doesn't want us to pray for each other. He knows that our prayer life is our most powerful weapon. That is why he fights our prayer life. Nevertheless, God wants us to stand our ground.

No matter what is going on in our lives, we must seek God's face. Most people are not confident that someone is calling their names out before God. Just as we appreciate someone praying for us, we should be praying for others.

Our lives have to mean something. It's not *how long* you live, but *how* you live. Dr. Myles Monroe's life was cut short, but he left a great legacy for us to remember. We all need to leave a legacy of something that will push someone toward God.

There should be no doubt as to whether or not you know God. If people don't know, whom will they go to in time of trouble? They need to know that our prayer lives can impact the heavens on their behalf. When they cannot find God, they need someone who knows God.

> *"I have set watchmen upon thy walls, O Jerusalem, which shall never hold their peace day nor night: ye that make mention of the LORD, keep not silence, And give him no rest, till he establish, and till he make Jerusalem a praise in the earth." – Isaiah 62:6–7*

The Lord is looking for men and women of God whom He can set in place as watchmen.

Accept Your Assignment as a Warrior

This is an elevated position. Set yourself as a prayer warrior. Don't back off because of circumstances or fear. Cry out day and night.

Sometimes, we minimize each other because of what we see on the surface, but many of us have an extraordinary anointing on our lives. It is not about large numbers. Most times God deals with a remnant. We are not average.

God is calling on us. He wants to do incredible things through us. Someone needs the Word of God from us. People are waiting for us. God is waiting for us to show up in our prayer closet. He needs to hear our voices.

Until we are *"a praise in the earth,"* we need to keep praying. It is better to pray until our last breath than worry until our last breath. Go out doing the will of God. God will use us or use someone else. We need to set our clocks to get up and go to our prayer post. Imagine the power of prayer: if one can put a thousand to flight. Let's believe that our reward is great when we seek the Lord.

If you are willing to accept your assignment as a warrior, stand up and take your place in God's army. It doesn't matter where your prayer life is. If you want to go higher, choose the high calling of a warrior.

Chapter Five

How Do I Apply and Pray?

*"Be wise in the way you act toward outsiders; make the most of every opportunity. Let your conversation be always full of grace, **seasoned with salt, so that you may know how to answer everyone.**" – Colossians 4:5–6 (NIV)*
(Emphasis mine)

Every day that passes, every week that goes by, something significant is happening to indicate that God is dealing with our nation and with the world. Sometimes, it looks like the devil is just running rampant.

Take, for example, the violence and rioting that occurred in Ferguson, Missouri. Not only was our entire nation sitting on the edge to discover what the verdict would be, but many in other nations were also waiting to hear the conclusion to this real-life drama. The result was almost a self-fulfilling prophecy.

From the corner barbershops of the inner city to the water coolers of Wall Street, Americans gathered to ponder the implications of this national tragedy. Sociologists weighed in as new developments mounted. Political analysts and pundits in our news outlets collectively deliberated on the potential consequences of the fatal shooting. What they prophesied was exactly what happened: news of the indictment traveled like the shot heard around the world. Protesters went wild. Looters, outfitted with bricks, busted car windows, ravaged storefronts, and demolished other people's property.

Armed with kerosene to burn buildings, rioters swarmed the streets. Prepared with gas masks, looters concealed their identities, sabotaged the police's crowd control efforts, and recklessly plundered neighborhood businesses. It was pre-planned violence and pre-planned pillaging everywhere.

The scenario was played out again when around the world people of all races witnessed the policeman's knee in the neck of George Floyd. The cries of the almost lifeless Floyd saying "I can't breathe" were heard in the media in every language worldwide.

It provoked nonviolent and violent protests in the streets of major cities throughout the United States. The chants of "Black Lives Matter", were louder than ever.

The violence increased as the days went by. Protesters of all colors and ages were crowded in the streets holding signs and wearing tee shirts that Black lives matter.

Protests didn't just surface in the state of Missouri or the streets of Minnesota, however. In Georgia, drivers stopped traffic on the expressway to communicate their anger about the indictment. A similar ripple effect emerged in Chicago. In St. Louis and California, consumers boycotted businesses and shut down trade for the day. Why? To send a message to the nation.

Subversive groups joined the ranks by Escalating the protests ie. throwing Molotov Cocktails, hurling bricks, and looting. There were many arrested and many injuries.

There were political demands to Defund the Police. Racial Injustice was on the mind of the whole world during the very height of the COVID 19 pandemic.

What Is the Church's Response?

As I observed all of the responses to this mayhem, my question was, "What was the response—not of the world, not of black people—but what was the response of the Church?" You're not going to find the Christian response to the crisis on Fox News. You're not going to find it on MSNBC. It's not going to be on CNN. Where should you go? People have called my church, asking, "How should we look at this? How should we deal with these issues?"

My answer: use the salt of the gospel to explain and heal the wounds of this world. When Christ's Church communicates the values and principles of God's kingdom as a way to address the tragedies and events of this earthly kingdom, the Church is, in essence, operating in God's prophetic voice to mankind. In Matthew 5:13 (PHILLIPS), Jesus explained to His disciples, *"You are the earth's salt. But if the salt should become tasteless, what can make it salt again? It is completely useless and can only be thrown out of doors and stamped underfoot."*

As Christians, we often underestimate the effectiveness of providing a clear, biblical view of life's calamities to a watching world. Yet the Church's declaration of Christ's salvation and example for mankind is the only viable soundbite that a despairing world—tuning in to the news media for answers—needs to hear. Let's take note of a statistic, contrasting the importance of a Christian's influence on today's society:

> *"Who's Who is a perennial publication that produces the names of people who have risen above the norm to make a positive impact on society. Research shows it takes 25,000 families of unskilled laboring background to produce one person in the annual Who's Who, it requires 10,000 skilled laboring families to put one person in Who's Who, 2,500 professional families are necessary to accomplish the same task, but only seven missionary families are needed to produce one member of Who's Who. Christian influence definitely adds salt to society."* [1]

Likewise, when I looked at Ferguson, my first question was, "Where was the Church?" When the Church responds and approaches the microphone, what is the Church saying? I'm listening to hear if this is the voice of God or if it is the Church giving a worldly response.

We must trumpet a prophetic response to this nation. We must engage our neighbors, coworkers, family members—whoever we notice is processing world issues—and explain to them what the Scriptures have to say about those issues and what God is requiring of them as a result.

---

[1] "Over the Top," Zig Ziglar, 1994.

I recently realized that Billy Graham did exactly that—declared more than just an evangelistic message but a prophetic message to our culture. And what I mean by a prophetic message is this: communicating a perspective that is supremely God's perspective (not man's opinion) regarding the tragedies, misfortunes, and challenges of our times and urging mankind to "do life" God's way.

We must first examine our own lives to make sure we are "doing life" God's way. Then our admonition will come from a position of authenticity and credibility.

As I was listening to a video of Billy Graham, he didn't simply deliver an evangelistic sermon. I was expecting the same basic "Just come to Jesus—come as you are" sermon. As I continued listening to him, he was giving a prophetic message to this nation! He dealt with every issue that was relevant at that time, challenging his audience to live for God. It didn't matter where he was. It didn't matter who his audience was. It didn't matter who the current president was. It didn't matter which political party was in power at the time. He stood for righteousness!

Now that Billy Graham has passed, the baton *has* to pass! There needs to be a prophetic voice—a voice that interprets a particular issue from God's perspective confronts any moral error related to that issue, and cautions the nation to change accordingly.

Applying the First Response to Crisis: Discerning Tragedy and the Body Accurately

In the previous chapters, I explained how Christians should react when "Fergusons" and "Columbines" and "September 11s" take the world off guard. Our immediate response should be to observe major catastrophes through a lens of discernment.

When any major shaking takes place in our lives, we need to ask if God might be trying to speak through it and then be willing to undergo any self-examination to discern if the Lord could be requiring anything of us.

When Jesus spent His last dinner with His closest friends, He announced the disturbing news that one of them would betray Him. This was a shocking statement—one that immediately shook them and brought them great distress. Interestingly enough, each disciple of Christ—one by one—asked the Lord for His assessment: "Is it I, Lord?" (Matthew 26:20-29) This is the type of response the Apostle Paul referred to when he admonished the church at Corinth to "discern the body" (1 Corinthians 11:29). Similarly, as we hear news of another shooting or another natural disaster, we must ask for the Lord's assessment of the situation.

Next, we must ascertain if there is any personal wrongdoing that we must repent of and change, thereby bringing subsequent and collective change to the nation. No longer are we going to be able to run and point the finger, declaring, "They're the problem!" Actually, "they" are not the problem. It starts with us. Judgment starts where? It begins in the house of God!

So, when there are situations that are going on all the time, over and over again, we need to ask why—because the Lord is trying to get our attention. Once He has our attention, we can inquire of God as the psalmist David did:

> *"Investigate my life, O God, find out everything about me; Cross-examine and test me, get a clear picture of what I'm about; See for yourself whether I've done anything wrong— then guide me on the road to eternal life." – Psalm 138:23–24 (MSG)*

Applying the Second Response to Crisis: Overcoming Fear

In addition to examining and interpreting the calamities of our day through the lens of Scripture, we must get past our fear. You cannot be a Christian and call yourself standing for Christ, yet react fearfully to the works of the devil. We can't be afraid. That's the strategy and scare tactic of terrorism. Terrorism jumps on your fear to keep you from moving!

Most Christians are afraid that someone's going to believe something untrue about them or that someone's not going to like them. You *will not be liked* if you're standing as a Christian. You need to understand that now.

When the riots broke out in Baltimore after the police brutality and subsequent death of Freddie Gray, a special thing occurred that the national news may not have broadcast but the local Baltimore news did. A group of about one-hundred local pastors showed up, locked arms, and marched in the streets amid the looting.

Once they had walked a certain distance, these pastors stopped in the middle of an intersection and got on their knees. With heads bowed and arms still locked, they prayed in the street. They risked their lives, got "in harm's way," and made a nonverbal declaration to a watching community that the Church was present in the midst of chaos—communicating care and providing prayer.

Trade the Expectation of Popularity for the Role of Watchman

> *"Son of man, I have made you a watchman for the people of Israel; so hear the word I speak and give them warning from me. When I say to the wicked, 'You wicked person, you will surely die,' and you do not speak out to dissuade them from their ways, that wicked person will die for their sin, and I will hold you accountable for their blood. But if you do warn the wicked person to turn from their ways and they do not do so, they will die for their sin, though you yourself will be saved." – Ezekiel 33:7–9 (NIV)*

This Scripture passage explains the role of the watchman, and that the watchman must *watch* and look for where the enemy is coming. Now, to be a watchman, you must also be familiar with what the enemy looks like! The enemy is not some white person. The enemy is not some black person.

We must understand that we wrestle not against flesh and blood. Do you understand that we're surveying the times as watchmen, and we're scouting to see what the devil's trying to do with this generation? What is the enemy trying to do to our young people? Why were our young people in the streets, throwing bricks and going on rampages regardless of their agreement with the Ferguson indictment? What was going on?

There was a spiritual power operating beneath the surface—the prince of the power of the air was leading people to incite violence! We need to prophetically declare who was behind all of this. The Bible refers to Satan in Ephesians 2:2 (AMP) as *"the prince of the power of the air, the spirit who is now at work in the disobedient [the unbelieving, who fight against the purposes of God]."* The New Living Translation calls the devil "the commander of the powers in the unseen world. He is the spirit at work in the hearts of those who refuse to obey God."

Whether it's the violence of Ferguson, the unjust treatment of blacks under apartheid, or the corruption within our police department—all abuse of power and corruption in the world is motivated by the prince of the power of the air, the spirit that is at work in those who are disobedient. Don't be surprised. Don't be shaken! We have to be bearers of the truth.

Man Your Post: The Prayer Closet

I'm calling you, watchmen! Man your posts!

Manning your post means you have to be in the right place at the right time. You have to have a designated time and place to pray every day. Your prayer closet is your power closet! If your closet could talk, would it even know you? I'm not talking about dresses. I'm not talking about getting clothes. I'm talking about using your closet as a regular, private place in your house to pray.

You may say, "I don't like going to corporate prayer at church on Friday night. I don't want to do that. I'm tired." Well, let me ask you a question: if you don't prefer to come to church to pray, where *do* you pray? Find someplace that you *do* pray and go man your post!

Those of us who are Christians cannot call ourselves born again and not be called into the Lord's service as warriors! God gives all of us a special assignment on the battlefield, but every one of us has an assignment to pray. It's not *if* you pray; it's *when* you pray! You have to man your post. There are people depending on your prayer life!

Identify Your Prayer Assignment

In order to man your post, you have to have a daily prayer assignment by God. You may say, "Daily?" Yes, daily! You have to go before God every day. You will not always know where God's going to take you in prayer, but that's what makes it so exciting! You should go into your prayer closet, asking the Lord, "What is my assignment today? Who do You want me to pray for?" Sometimes, you don't even feel the release to pray for yourself! You may have a *long* list of needs to pray about, and enter into your prayer time yet never wind up praying for yourself—because that was *not* your prayer assignment from God for that day!

Watch

So, you must man your post, identify your prayer assignment from God, and then watch. The term "watch" in the Scriptures didn't refer to looking at something, but it referred to a designated time of the day. The watch could be in the noon hour, or it could be in the evening. Whatever the case, there was a watch allotted by time.

What time have you allotted for daily prayer? Convenience shouldn't govern whether or not you pray. You have to set a fixed time when you're going to pray each day. You have to make the decision: "I'm going to pray in the morning. I'm going to cut the television off. I'm going to go to bed early." Do whatever it takes to man your watch at the right time!

The Watchman's Warning

In Ezekiel 33:6 the prophet warns of what will happen when the watchman remains silent:

> *"But if the watchman sees the sword coming and does not blow the trumpet to warn the people and the sword comes and takes someone's life, that person's life will be taken because of their sin, but I will hold the watchman accountable for their blood." – Ezekiel 33:6 (NIV)*

Sometimes, I wonder how responsible and culpable is the Church for all the murder, bloodshed, and sin that is going on in this world. How many national and world tragedies took place without warning from a watchman? No one stepped forward ahead of time and warned the leaders or the people involved about the consequences and the penalties of their iniquity.

Once a person warns someone, then he's free from any responsibility! When it's all said and done, he can say, "I'm good!" Why? Because he *warned* them, even though they did not heed the warning. If a person doesn't warn others and simply allows them to remain at risk, then that person isn't serving as a watchman.

For all of us who are Christians, that means we can't let individuals stay in the same state they were. We have to confront them at least *one time*, warning them in earnest: "If you stay on this pathway, it will be a path leading to hell. But Jesus can save you. He can change your life right now. Don't you want me to pray for you?"

We must step forward and say that because if they die and we haven't warned them, their blood is on our hands! What's even greater is if they've been taken over by satan and die in their iniquity, the guilt of their blood is on our hands. That's a sobering thought. We could wish that Ezekiel 33 could just drop out of your Bible. Unfortunately, the Bible doesn't let us slip and slide on this mandate. God is looking for a watchman. Become that watchman!

Prayer and Passion for God's House

Let's consider Mark 11:15–17 (KJV):

"And they come to Jerusalem: and Jesus went into the temple, and began to cast out them that sold and bought in the temple, and overthrew the tables of the moneychangers, and the seats of them that sold doves; and would not suffer that any man should carry any vessel through the temple. And he taught, saying unto them, 'Is it not written, My house shall be called of all nations the house of prayer? but ye have made it a den of thieves.'"

You may not be selling doves. You may not be considered money changers. But what do you think the Lord's attitude is toward congregations whose primary focus is entertainment? They think that it's more important to entertain the congregants than it is to provide the Word of God.

What about those who are manipulators? You might have encountered them or seen them on television. They engineer their church services in such a way that their parishioners feel pressured to give all their money to the church.

What about those who are self-serving? They are not living godly lives, but they're telling others to live godly lives. They are hypocrites.

What about churches that function like corporate businesses? They gain from their people, but they do not care for their people.

What about houses of worship that are nothing more than celebrity worship?

I'm telling you right now, God's not happy with the churches that are like that! I'm going to go one step further—Jesus disrupted the business of the temple because He had a passion for His Church. Remember what He said: "*My* house will be called a house of prayer!" (Matthew 21:13) He personalized this issue!

The Old Testament addressed how God's people gave more attention to their own houses than to God's house. They were committing their time, money, and best efforts to decking the halls of their showcase homes, yet they neglected the most important house. God forewarned that He would make their lives like bags filled with holes.

> *"Then came the word of the LORD by Haggai the prophet, saying, Is it time for you, O ye, to dwell in your cieled houses, and this house lie waste? Now therefore thus saith the LORD of hosts; Consider your ways. Ye have sown much, and bring in little; ye eat, but ye have not enough; ye drink, but ye are not filled with drink; ye clothe you, but there is none warm; and he that earneth wages earneth wages to put it into a bag with holes." – Haggai 1:3–6*

Because God's people were forsaking the house of the Lord, they were not prospering in their personal lives. Their priorities were all wrong. Such is the predicament of those who don't contribute to the prosperity of God's house—they won't prosper if they don't help God's house to prosper!

Some believe they don't need to physically go to church as long as they give their regular tithes to their home church. Here's my question to them: Is that really your house? Is that the way you would tend to and care for your personal house? Are you passionate about your personal house but not about God's house?

For the gospel's sake, first-century Christians poured everything at the apostles' feet. They sold houses and lands so that ministry could go forth. What's the priority of His house to you? The church has to be full of prayer warriors, not the self-serving and worldly. We're not in here to look like the world. We are here to receive those who are *from* the world. Oh, how we need God to bring regeneration and newness and freshness and healing in the house of God!

Keeping Watch with Jesus

As watchmen, we must enter our prayer closets and man our post daily. As watchmen, we must identify the priorities and assignments that God has chosen for us and pray. And as watchmen, we must determine in our hearts that we will stay committed to intercession for the long haul.

In Luke 18:1, Jesus taught "...men ought always to pray, and not to faint." The Apostle Paul urged the church at Thessalonica to pray without ceasing (1 Thessalonians 5:17). In the Garden of Gethsemane during Jesus's darkest hour, He challenged His disciples, "Are you so utterly unable to stay awake and keep watch with Me for one hour?" (Matthew 26:40, AMPC).

I thought about that question Jesus asked His disciples when He needed them most.

"Lord," I entreated, "help me to have the desire, the focus, and the stamina I need to pray for at least one hour."

Then it occurred to me that Jesus was not only mentioning the *duration* of prayer in that Scripture verse but the *terms* of prayer—that it would be accomplished *with Him*!

Why would Jesus, the Son of the Almighty God, the all-sufficient God who needs nothing nor no one, ask those three disciples to pray with Him? Even though He is God, Jesus needed someone to pray with Him. There's a multiplication of power when we pray with others: one can put one thousand to flight and two can put ten thousand to flight (Leviticus 26:8). There's something about our corporate prayer that has power! There is power in our agreement over the petitions we bring to God.

As we reflect on the Ferguson riots, the church must respond with a prophetic voice to our nation that cuts through all the rhetoric and public relation sound bites and gives the world answers from God's perspective. The prophet Isaiah lived during an era of national unrest and injustice—much like the times we're experiencing in America—and he spoke to his people with a relevant, poignant challenge:

> *"Listen! The LORD's arm is not too weak to save you, nor is his ear too deaf to hear you call. It's your sins that have cut you off from God. Because of your sins, he has turned away and will not listen anymore. Your hands are the hands of murderers, and your fingers are filthy with sin. Your lips are full of lies, and your mouth spews corruption."*
>
> *"No one cares about being fair and honest. The people's lawsuits are based on lies. They conceive evil deeds and then give birth to sin." – Isaiah 59:1–4 (NLT)*

The tragedy of Ferguson is not only that there were lives lost and a city ravaged but also that there was a moment missed. The debates surrounding the case failed to acknowledge the wrongdoing of African Americans as well as police officers. The prophet Isaiah did not overlook his own people's culpability when addressing the problems of his nation.

The protestors of Ferguson must acknowledge that they do evil things within their community, yet they protest about the evil done to them. They are killing their own people as a result of gang warfare, everyday street crimes, and drug deals, yet they cry out for justice when someone of *another* race kills their people.

The cries for justice in Ferguson need to be answered with, "Examine your wrongdoing before complaining of the police's wrongdoing." The prophetic response to the lawbreakers looting in the streets, setting cars on fire, and killing their neighbors should be what Isaiah's words were in verse 4:

> *"No one cares about being fair and honest. The people's lawsuits are based on lies. They conceive evil deeds and then give birth to sin."*

They claim that "black lives matter," but there is no concern for life because they're shooting their own people.

Isaiah spoke of a national consequence that has also plagued our communities.

> *"So there is no justice among us, and we know nothing about right living. We look for light but find only darkness. We look for bright skies but walk in gloom. We grope like the blind along a wall, feeling our way like people without eyes. Even at brightest noontime, we stumble as though it were dark. Among the living, we are like the dead. We growl like hungry bears; we moan like mournful doves. We look for justice, but it never comes. We look for rescue, but it is far away from us." – Isaiah 59:19–11 (NLT)*

The prophetic voice of the Church needs to warn these cities in crisis that if they continue in their sinful ways and don't repent, they will become so blind that they will grope for answers yet never figure out how to get themselves out of their predicament. They will look for rescue, but it will be far away from them.

What our country doesn't understand is that there is a darkness and gloom that follows any continued, prolonged practice of sin. Until a community renounces its contribution to the evil in its midst, they will look for light but only find darkness. They will look for bright skies but only find gloom.

It has been reported that during the three- or four-week period of the Ferguson riots, the black-on-black murder rate increased in Chicago. Meanwhile, "White America," perplexed by this irony, was asking, "What is all the fuss about black lives matter in Ferguson? Who is going over to Chicago to tell the black people there to stop killing each other?"

> *"And judgment is turned away backward, and justice standeth afar off: for truth is fallen in the street, and equity cannot enter." – Isaiah 59:14*

The black protestors of Ferguson, Missouri, were crying out for justice, but interestingly, they were not crying out for judgment. The people didn't really want true justice but specifically their interpretation of a justice that will benefit them and will result in no judgment or consequences for their part in the calamity.

The prophet Isaiah had noted that "truth is fallen in the street." After the verdict in the case of Michael Brown, black protesters stormed into the streets, crying out for truth surrounding his death, but in actuality, no one was concerned about the truth because they would not acknowledge that Michael Brown made the first move of violence, not the police officer. In my opinion, the truth didn't matter to the protesters. What mattered to the protesters was that a black guy was shot. Therefore, the Truth was cast down in the street.

Consequently, if Truth gets cast down in the streets, then there can be no equity or justice. If they're going to negate the truth (not admit that Michael Brown was aggressive and hit the officer first), then (according to Isaiah 59) they can't have fairness. It was a lawsuit and publicity campaign based on lies.

Understandably, African Americans are angry about a history of repeated racial injustices that have occurred over the years. It is true that the judicial system has not been working for the black community. Yet the question remains, "What's the *Christian* response in the midst of it?" Yes, the public was looking for justice, but they were denying the truth. Therefore, "justice stood far off, truth fell in the streets, and equity could not even enter."

So, what's the solution to the dilemma? It's the same solution that Isaiah described to his people centuries ago.

> *"...and the LORD saw it, and it displeased him that there was no judgment. And he saw that there was no man, and wondered that there was no intercessor..." – Isaiah 59:15b–16a*

The Lord saw that there wasn't anyone willing to intervene in a dire situation. No one was interceding and praying for the crisis.

Now, I ask the same thing regarding our day and time: is there anybody in the midst of all this sin and looting who will pray? Why is there no intercessor?

The watchman is the solution! As we learned in an earlier chapter, the watchman is up high, looking out to protect the people and looking to see when the enemy is coming and what the enemy is doing. His post is to watch. His job is to intercede. The watchman's duty is to watch and pray so that we are not ignorant of the enemy's strategies.

The intercessor sees the sin of the people and goes to God and confesses sin on behalf of the people...even if the people don't know that they're guilty. The intercessor takes responsibility for the Church, allowing the sin to grow to the point that it has grown.

> *"Blow the ram's horn in Jerusalem! Announce a time of fasting; call the people together for a solemn meeting. Gather all the people—the elders, the children, and even the babies. Call the bridegroom from his quarters and the bride from her private room. Let the priests, who minister in the LORD's presence, stand and weep between the entry room to the Temple and the altar. Let them pray, 'Spare your people, LORD! Don't let your special possession become an object of mockery. Don't let them become a joke for unbelieving foreigners who say, "Has the God of Israel left them?" Then the LORD will pity his people and jealously guard the honor of his land." – Joel 2:15–17 (NLT)*

Prayer is a decision. You're called to be a watchman.

Chapter Six

Flip-Flop Morality

We have protest marches, but we also need another "p"—prayer. We need to be organizing *prayer* marches, in addition, to protest marches because nothing of lasting value is going to take place in our country unless somebody cries out to God. Someone has to cry out to God for His mercy, for His justice, and for His judgment. Someone needs to cry out to God for His grace and favor to come upon this nation.

> *"A person's own folly leads to their ruin, yet their heart rages against the LORD." – Proverbs 19:3 (NIV)*

We hear protesters declaring, "Black lives matter!" This is kind of ironic though because *every* life matters! Yet protesters are leading the public to believe that a life only matters when a white police officer takes a black man's life. But if a black man takes another black man's life, does *that life* matter?

I'm not minimizing the fact that in many cases, our law enforcement arrives at a crime scene already predisposed to believe that the black person involved has done something wrong. There are differences in how a police officer may react to a black person versus a white person, but if we're going to start publicizing that black lives matter; let's also publicize that a black life in the womb matters as well. Our nation's black leaders are operating from a double standard in regards to the sanctity of human life. Let's steer the debate to help black people acknowledge that black unborn babies also matter to God!

Here is a grave irony of the Black Lives Matter Movement: the same people protesting that black lives matter will undergo an abortion or support it, taking the life of an innocent black baby and never concluding that anything's wrong with it.

Here's another irony of the Black Lives Matter Movement: the same people who are crashing windows in protest of black lives being taken by white police officers will take a black life *themselves* if someone crosses them the wrong way. Yet "black lives matter."

No one wants to see a black man killed. I don't want to see our young men and women going to prison. I don't want to see black people dying of AIDS. I don't want to see a generation of black babies dying in the womb.

As a race of people, African Americans lead in every area of death and degeneration. Our demographic statistics soar in the areas of abortion, AIDS, black-on-black crime, incarceration, heart disease, hypertension, and diabetes. The ratio is higher for African Americans to live in single-parent households, in poverty, and in juvenile detention than any other demographic. Our education is lower, and our drop-out rates are higher.

Murder in the womb—we lead. What about protesting "black lives matter" for black babies in the womb?

We're upset that Garner's life was snuffed out even as he was yelling, "I can't breathe!" But what does a child say when he's sucked out of the womb through abortion? He, too, is saying, "I can't breathe!" But it's okay for our convenience because we say, "I don't have time for a baby." You had time to produce the baby. You made time for that. But you don't have time to raise a baby. If black lives matter, that black baby's life should matter enough to you to raise him or her.

The Church—the body of Christ—must scripturally frame the discussions about today's issues to ensure that our culture is processing current events and debates from a biblical perspective. Instead of repeating what the protesters are shouting, the people of God must lead the way to the solutions. We can't just follow suit because following suit with the world is not finishing the discussion. The Church is called to frame the discussions, and the Church is called to pray and seek God for the solutions.

When black clergy are given the opportunity to go on the air and address the problems of our day, it is rare to find them confronting the real problem. When the media puts a mic in front of their face, they're not calling the black community to repentance nor are they calling the nation to repentance. What we need are prophetic Christians who will address the ungodliness and wickedness of this nation that is pushing us further from God. We have to call our nation back to God.

Those who consider themselves to be the black community's spiritual leaders shouldn't just jump in front of the "Black Lives Matter" movement so they can get arrested and credential themselves as activists. No, they need to declare the truth. This world, this nation, needs a prophetic word from God.

We need a prophetic word from God because in today's society, what's wrong is called right, and what's right is called wrong. A good example of this "flip-flop morality" is the firing involving Atlanta's former fire chief, Kelvin Cochran. He's a tremendous man. He was hired during former Atlanta Mayor Shirley Franklin's administration. He was so good that former President Barack Obama promoted him to oversee fire policy and administration for the entire country.

He spent about a year as U.S. Fire Administrator but returned to Atlanta (upon request by Mayor Kasim Reed, who succeeded Franklin) to oversee Atlanta's fire and rescue department. Ironically, the mayor who asked Chief Cochran to return to Atlanta wound up firing him because of stances he took in a book he wrote for his men's Bible study entitled *Who Told You that You Were Naked?*[2]

As a devout Christian, Cochran was trying to strengthen the men in his church and provide a biblical view of sexuality and the sanctity of marriage, so he put this book together. In it, he addressed adultery, fornication, uncleanliness, lasciviousness, idolatry, witchcraft, hatred, various emulations, wraths, strife, heresy, envy, murder, and drunkenness. Cochran specifically defined uncleanness as "whatever is opposite of purity, including sodomy, homosexuality, lesbianism, bestiality, and other forms of sexual perversion." The book wound up in the hands of coworkers, and news of it reached homosexual activists, who were outraged by Cochran's biblical convictions. What

---

[2] https://www.afa.net/action-alerts/stand-with-fire-chief-kelvin-cochran/

happened next developed into a vocational nightmare for Cochran and a political controversy that went viral.

The LBGT community was enraged. They pressured Atlanta Mayor Kasim Reed, who responded, "I want to be clear that the material in Chief Cochran's book is not representative of my personal beliefs."[3] Homosexual activists were upset that Chief Cochran described homosexuality as being equal to bestiality! They protested and pressured the mayor's office until Chief Cochran was suspended and later fired.

In a written statement, Mayor Reed announced that Cochran was not sensitive to the various beliefs of those in his administration and, therefore, was not worthy to oversee the fire department.

Atlanta City Councilman Alex Wan, who is openly gay, agreed with the termination, stating, "When you're a city employee, and [your] thoughts, beliefs, and opinions are different from the city's, you have to check them at the door."[4]

So, follow that out. "A Christian can never be in leadership," is what they were communicating. The irony is that this was a black mayor who suspended Cochran (a black man) without pay and later fired him. So, in the larger scheme of things, they were communicating that unrighteousness is more important than blackness. Let's call it like it is—it's not black versus white; it's righteousness versus unrighteousness. That's the story right there. That's what we're dealing with. The LGBT community had political clout with the mayor, who needed their support for reelection. Therefore, that black man had to go down, and the LGBT won.

What the prophet Isaiah declared centuries ago is still true today:

"Our courts oppose the righteous, and justice is nowhere to be found. Truth stumbles in the streets, and honesty has been outlawed. Yes, truth is gone, and anyone who renounces evil is attacked." – Isaiah 59:14-15a (NLT)

---

[3] Ibid.

[4] Ibid.

When I learned about Chief Cochran's unjust treatment and religious persecution by the government, I contacted him and assured him that he had support from the body of Christ. I met with him often and prayed with him. I (and others) held press conferences to denounce the injustice of his termination and expose it as religious persecution.

This is the first Christian response to a crisis. We should view the current controversy through the lens of Scripture and declare to a watching world what God's Word says about the issue.

Despite the political firestorm, Chief Cochran remained steadfast. "I'm not discouraged, and I'm not downtrodden," he said. "This is a God thing, and He's going to do great things, and He will vindicate me publicly."[5] His courageous stand for truth is the second Christian response to a crisis: refusing to fear.

A group called Georgia Equality declares that it's okay for a man to have sex with a man, and it's okay for a woman to have sex with a woman. Let me tell you something right now: a line is being drawn in the sand. Jesus said you're either for Me or you're against Me (Matthew 12:30). There's no other position.

> *"Even them will I bring to my holy mountain, and make them joyful in my house of prayer: their burnt offerings and their sacrifices shall be accepted upon mine altar; for mine house shall be called an house of prayer for all people." – Isaiah 56:7 (KJV)*

"The holy mountain" in this verse depicts God's presence. He wants to bring you to that holy place. His desire is to commune with you, spend time with you, and bring you away from the world to Himself.

Many times, even when Jesus went into the wilderness, He drew away from the people, so we get the imagery in this passage of God bringing you away unto Himself. He said seek Me early, you shall find Me (Proverbs 8:17).

Also in Isaiah 56:7, God said He would "make them joyful." It almost seems like it's a dichotomy to say that He will make us joyful

---

[5] Todd Starnes, *Todd's American Dispatch*, "Atlanta Fire Chief: I was fired because of my Christian faith," FoxNews.com, Published January 07, 2015.

because there should be anguish and concern about the direction our nation is going. Yet the Lord still wants us to have a spirit of joy as we serve Him in such perilous times! Why? Because God knows the end from the beginning, and He has revealed in His Word how everything will end. We know we're on the right team—the winning side!

If you were in a fight or playing in a championship game and knew you were going to win, you wouldn't mind the hits. You wouldn't mind the pressure. You wouldn't mind the tribulation because you would know you're going to win! The joy of the Lord is your strength. So, be joyful because you're rejoicing about the end.

Next, Isaiah continues, "in my house of prayer." Prayer has to be the priority of the Church. There should be more hours of prayer than preaching. More hours of prayer than singing. More hours of prayer than music, childcare, or anything else.

In my local church, the Father's House, we have had 5:00 a.m. prayer two hours a day, seven days a week; and every first Friday, we've had intercessory prayer from 9:00 p.m. until 11:00 p.m. There's more prayer going on than anything else. Because Jesus said, My church shall be what?—a house of prayer. We must have our priorities right. We can't minimize prayer.

I was looking at Isaiah 62, and I realized that the Lord was clear about showing Israel what His call was for them:

"And they shall call them, The holy people, The redeemed of the LORD*: and thou shalt be called, Sought out, A city not forsaken." – Isaiah 62:12*

The Lord was encouraging Israel: "Yes, you've gone through some things, but you belong to Me. I've got your back." Ultimately, when we stand for Him, we're going to win every time.

Remember, the Apostle Paul went through all kinds of troubles. He was shipwrecked. He was beaten. He was robbed. He was cold. He was hungry. He had experienced just about everything imaginable. He was a man of high stature. He was trained in the best of the Hebrew. Very few people exceeded his level of understanding and knowledge, but he was treated like the scum of the earth. Yet even while he was in prison, he wrote letters that we're still reading today. His test became his testimony.

Understand this: we have to maintain hope. Even in our prayers, we have to be hopeful. The Bible says that faith is the substance of things hoped for; the evidence of things not seen (Hebrews 11:1). The core of faith has to look toward something. It's the substance of things *hoped* for. So, you cannot have true faith without hope. Therefore, your prayers cannot be effective unless they are filled with hope.

God said that without faith, it's impossible to please Him. The very nature of faith is that you have to have hope. If you are hopeless, you are dead because hopelessness brings on depression. It brings on anxiety. And it eventually brings a spirit of death. But hope brings life.

Hope is not based on what you see. If you have to see it, it's not hope. Romans 8:24–25 says this:

> *"For we are saved by hope: but hope that is seen is not hope: for what a man seeth, why doth he yet hope for? But if we hope for that we see not, then do we with patience wait for it."*

When we look at this generation or look at the problems and the systemic evil that we're dealing with, we must recognize that God is the God of government. He's put this thing in place. He's going to have the last word over it. Our job is to preach His Word.

Chapter Seven

Whose Kingdom is It?

*"And to Him was given dominion, Glory and a kingdom,
That all the peoples, nations and men of every language
Might serve Him. His dominion is an everlasting dominion
Which will not pass away; and His kingdom is one Which
will not be destroyed." – Daniel 7:14 (NASB)*

We are in the midst of an international crisis, and recurring police killings and brutality reports all around the country are further exacerbating our national crisis.

Take, for example, the arrest and unfortunate death of Eric Garner, an African-American father of six, street-vending on the corners of Staten Island, New York. Suspecting Garner of illegally peddling untaxed cigarettes, a white NYC police officer arrested him, used excessive force, and choked Garner into unconsciousness, resulting in his eventual death.

Later, the New York City Medical Examiner's Office ruled his death as a homicide by illegal chokehold.[6] Yet a grand jury decided not to indict the NYPD officer who killed Garner. The verdict sparked local vigils demanding justice for Eric Garner and nation-wide non-violent protests, demonstrations, and rallies denouncing police brutality.[7]

---

[6] Dianis, Judith Browne. "Eric Garner was killed by more than just a chokehold," MSNBC.com., August 5, 2014.

[7] "The Death of Eric Garner, Wikipedia.com

Ironically, the grand jury's decline to indict the white officer killing Eric Garner[8] came roughly one week after a grand jury found no criminality in the actions of the white police officer who shot and killed Michael Brown in Ferguson, Missouri.

To add insult to injury, a few months later, Americans would mourn another unwarranted police killing. Tamir Rice, a twelve-year-old black boy, was pointing an airsoft gun at people in a recreation center in Cleveland, Ohio. A white police officer arrived on the scene, unaware that the youth did not have a real gun, and shot him. Public outcry broke out in Cleveland and waves of outrage reverberated around the country. Once again, the shooting gained national and international media coverage, fueling the "Black Lives Matter" movement.

What should our response be to things like this?

In the earlier chapters, we discussed the Church's role in providing discernment and biblical explanations to a watching world. We covered the desperate need we have for a prophetic voice to address the crises all around us.

Secondly, I encouraged the Church of Jesus Christ to courageously rise up and kick into action with no reservations and no fear.

I also talked to you about how important it is that we man our posts as intercessors and stand in the gap for the protection and the redemption of our nation.

Now, I want to talk to you about the Church's next reaction to crisis.

Response #5: We Have to Preach the Word of God and Conquer the World

Why is it so critical in this day and age to preach the word of God and conquer the world? Because we now live in a global society that

---

[8] Goodman, J. David and Baker, Al. "Wave of Protests After Grand Jury Doesn't Indict Officer in Eric Garner Chokehold Case," NY Times.com, December 3, 2014.

technology has united and brought people all over the world within reach.

Due to the invention of the Internet, Skype, cell phones, and other wireless technologies, events can occur and be instantaneously shared around the world. The shootings that take place at our front door can show up at Australia's back door, and people around the world are beginning to respond to what's going on around us.

The Washington Post reported that Russia's Foreign Ministry—commenting on the Ferguson incident—criticized Americans, accusing the United States of positioning itself as "a bastion of human rights" while being actively engaged in "serious violations of basic human rights and barbaric practices". Can you imagine this? Russia? A government with a long history of human rights atrocities has challenged the United States to uphold our morality! He's absolutely right though. We've left ourselves so vulnerable because we've moved away from any moral standard for life. So, now is the time for the preaching of the gospel to conquer the world.

We bring the world close to us through spheres of influence—the five areas of influence that you can govern.

The first area of government is your self-government. We can't call others into account for misusing their authority if we're misusing our own authority because the first control is self-control. You can't even govern yourself unless you have a Bible—a standard by which to live—and this becomes the way to love, the reason for your life, and everything centers on it.

The second area of government is family governance. As for me and my house, we will serve the Lord. That's the foundation for governing a family. We live by the Bible. We stand by the Bible. Our children need to understand prayer from an early age, and they'll learn it by seeing you praying. How in the world are they going to know how to pray if they don't hear it? They will establish every standard for life, based on what is allowed or experienced in the home.

Third, God is the governing head not only of the family but also of the Church. God is the final authority on everything that goes on in the family and everything that goes on in the Church.

Now, the world fights against God because the world makes man the measure of all things. Man's opinion becomes the standard for political correctness, tolerance, and ethics. Man's opinion determines what's okay and what's not. That's why the world goes to the media for answers and not the Church. But once we made man the standard for our behavior instead of God's Word, our nation began to tolerate more evil and ungodliness. So, what was wrong in the past is now determined to be right.

But know this: God is supreme over all thoughts and all opinions. What He says goes! So, the true standard must be, is it consistent with the Word of God? Don't ever let anybody try to deceive you: God is the measure of all things. He is our standard, not the world.

The first thing the devil tries to accomplish in every church is rebellion against authority. We grumble and complain about the pastor or about his message or about his convictions. "Man, I didn't like the message. And then he wants us to pray! I don't want to pray either! Read the Bible? I don't feel like reading the Bible every day!" We elevate ourselves above our leadership.

So, God says order in every area (1 Corinthians 14:40). If we disagree with something that is truly illegitimate, God will deal with unrighteous leadership even in the Church. However, you don't want to be the one who puts yourself in a position against God's authority—unless you want to be called Miriam or Aaron.

The fourth area of government is civil government. Christians are increasingly being kicked out of civil government. Why? Because there's no tolerance for the Christian worldview. But all civil government comes from God. So, even when somebody gets into office and is unrighteous, God's going to deal with their misuse of authority in civil government because it's His authority.

When the righteous are in authority, the people rejoice. However, God will allow His people to go under ungodly captivity as a punishment for sin—like when a nation starts to serve other gods or starts putting somebody before Him. So, if you mess with God long enough, part of His judgment will be to put you under ungodly, unrighteous, evil authority. We may ask, "Lord, how did this happen?" But the right question to ask is, "How did it happen in the church?" Because God's judgment first starts in the church!

The last area of government is in your vocations. Understand that in all these areas, the Lord is watching for you to declare the lordship of Christ. Whether you are an assistant or a garbage collector, you need to declare and reflect the glory of God in that area.

I mentioned in the previous chapter that Atlanta's former fire chief, Kelvin Cochran, came under attack for the stand he took in his book regarding homosexuality and the sins and perversions that are mentioned in Scripture. The homosexual community was offended and said, "He's lining us up with bestiality." Well, he didn't line them up with bestiality—the Bible lined them up with bestiality! Kelvin Cochran responded, "As a fire chief who's committed to God, I'm looking to cultivate an atmosphere to the glory of God!"

If you think about it, that's what we're saying when we say our pledge of allegiance. One nation under God, indivisible—what we're doing is declaring godliness. That's why we have chaplains in the Senate. Our country understood from the beginning that we want God's blessings.

But our government turned that around on Chief Cochran and said, "Oh, you want to cultivate the glory of God in your business? What does that mean? You're trying to make us what you are!" God's not going to stand for that. When you find somebody who's trying to live righteously, it's up to us to stand with him. Because if you don't stand, eventually somebody will have *your* number, and nobody will stand for you.

The late Pastor Otis Lockett from Greensboro, North Carolina, who regularly spoke at New Generation Ministries conferences, used to say, "We're going to wage a national takeover! We're going to stage a national takeover!" We as Christians have to stage a national takeover! We can't be passive about this. And it's exciting because we know we win. Greater is He that's within me than he that's within the world. I have the greater power working on my behalf! Jesus says to us, *"Go into all the world and preach the gospel to all creation" (Mark 16;15).*

That's every creature. *Everybody* has to hear the Word of God! We must put a premium on the preached word. There must be consistency in preaching the Word of God and declaring His truth. We are proclaimers of truth.

You may say, "I'm a little bashful." Well, you can be bashful and the devil will beat you up. Let me ask you a question: does the devil exempt you from his attack because you're bashful? My personality isn't an aggressive one. I'm a passive person. Is it possible that the devil will come up to my passivity and wear me out? Yes! So, you have to stay on the offensive.

When we talk about preaching the gospel, we're talking about witnessing to people, having a love for souls. Winning souls is the enemy's main line of attack because every person who is won to Christ, every person who becomes a disciple, every person who follows God because of you, has been snatched from the enemy.

Everywhere we go, some people are deceived, people who don't know, people who have honestly never heard the gospel. Some have heard, and they've walked away. Some have been brought into the things of God, but they've gone back. Yet it might be the seed of the word from your mouth that might be the right time, the right moment, that will make the right difference in their life. Preach the word to all the world and every creature. He that believes and is baptized will be saved.

Then you have these other great things:

> *"And these signs shall follow them that believe; In my name they shall out devils; they shall speak with new tongues; They shall take up serpents; and if they drink any deadly thing, it shall not hurt them; they shall lay hands on the sick, and they shall recover...And they went forth, and preached every where, and the Lord working with them, and confirming the word with signs following. Amen" – Mark 16:17–18, 20*

We've got to have a national takeover. The Bible says in Genesis 1:26 to take dominion, be fruitful, multiply—to dominate. We have to dominate.

I started looking around at what ISIS was doing, and I began to notice what their vision was. These guys have the vision to take over all of the Middle East. They started off talking about Iraq and Syria as their vision when they recruited members to their movement. But then they started calling themselves ISIL, which means the Islamic State of Iraq and the Levant. They changed their name so the public wouldn't know who they are and what they really stand for.

They started as a revolutionary movement, and then their vision changed to world domination, which is what ISIL—their new name— really means.

The terrorist militants plan first to extend their so-called Islamic caliphate into Eastern Europe, including Romania, Bulgaria, and Greece, and conquer as far as Austria, the entire Middle East, North Africa, Central Asia, Pakistan, and Afghanistan. And, of course, Turkey and Iran are also marked on ISIL's map.

And let me just say this: they're talking about the total annihilation of Israel. This is their goal! We haven't seen anything like this since Hitler. They plan to take over in five years. The first enemy that they have is Israel and the US. You think they're not here already? That's an international takeover.

What irony! As Christians, we're afraid to say we want to take over the world because we'll be accused of being narrow-minded crusaders and proselytizers. Jesus was clear about what the church's vision should be. He wanted Christians to take over the world! We should not be apologetic about this goal but *bold* about this goal! ISIL is not afraid to declare their vision for world domination.

But read Matthew 28:18–20 (NIV):

> *"Then Jesus came to them and said, 'All authority in heaven and on earth has been given to me. Therefore go and make disciples of all nations, baptizing them in the name of the Father and of the Son and of the Holy Spirit, and teaching them to obey everything I have commanded you. And surely I am with you always, to the very end of the age.'"*

Jesus says, "You go. You have the power. Go teach them." So, we have to teach people how to live. What we have has to influence other people. We are supposed to be on the offensive, in taking the gospel to the ends of the earth. The church has to have an offensive posture in regards to any crisis it encounters.

We are supposed to influence every area of life with the gospel of Jesus Christ and have a biblical frame to operate in their fields of endeavor so the world has a clear representation of Jesus on the earth.

So, let me ask you a question: who do you influence right now? Who can you influence with the message of the gospel?

The next thing I want to give you is a message of hope. The Bible says that faith is the substance of things hoped for and the evidence of things not seen (Hebrews 11:1). Our message is not "if you don't come to Jesus, you'll go to hell." Our message is "if you come to Him, He'll give you eternal life." Recognize that even in my words to you, it cannot be so hard that you don't have hope.

Please watch your words. Stop calling things as you see them. Call things that be not, the Bible says, as though they were (Romans 4:17). Call those things that you're believing for as though they were. Let's go further. Abraham *"...who against hope believed in hope, that he might become the father of many nations, according to that which was spoken, So shall thy seed be"* (Romans 4:18).

Even when it looks hopeless, against all hopelessness, you believe in hope! If God has spoken it, it's my reality. We hold the power. We have the power ourselves. We can do this. We don't have to let ISIS outdo us. They're dealing in the natural with natural weapons. We have spiritual weapons.

Jesus said just speak those things that you desire when you pray; believe that you receive them and you shall have them (Mark 11:24)! He didn't even tell you that you have to qualify it. He said even those things that you desire—get your desires in line with Him—and He will fulfill the desires of your heart. We have the advantage.

Now, remember Abraham was getting old. Yet *"...being not weak in faith..."* (Romans 4:19a). Don't be a faith weakling! There's just no excuse for it. You might say," Well, my circumstances are bad." So what? You still don't have to be weak in faith. When God calls you, He wants to say, "...thou good and faithful servant..." (Matthew 25:21a).

There's no excuse for crashing under circumstances. You may ask, why? Because my God is real. My God is able. My God is still on the throne. My God hasn't given up on me, and I'm not giving up on Him. I don't care what the situation is. I refuse to give up on the living God of all creation. I'd rather die believing than die in unbelief!

When there was no reason for hoping, Abraham hoped. Abraham said that when he was about one-hundred years old. How's he going to be the father of many nations at one-hundred years old? And Sarah's womb was dead. So, there was nothing in the natural that would make Abraham believe that this thing was happening, so he just had to hope. Sarah was laughing at him, but it doesn't matter if your spouse is laughing at you. Let them laugh! Believe in God—holding onto what He has said.

In Romans 8, the Apostle Paul talks about how hope is not even what you see. You have to believe God for something that you can't see. Faith is something that you don't have any clue how it's going to come to pass—the evidence of things not seen.

In Romans 4:20 it says Abraham *"...staggered not at the promises of God through unbelief; but was strong in faith, giving glory to God...."* Even in the most unlikely possibility, Abraham said, "I'm not going to stagger. I'm going to walk strong in faith. I'm taking major steps. I'm believing God. I'm not going to waver at all! And I'm going to be giving glory to God as I'm going. I'm going to give Him praise because I know He's real."

Defy the devil by your words! Defy the devil by your belief! He's the father of lies! He's deceiving people. He's even deceiving the church. You know the truth. Hold fast to it.

Romans 4:21 says, *"And being fully persuaded that, what he had promised, he was able also perform."* Abraham was fully persuaded. There's no room for doubt. There's no room for unbelief—not here!

Fully persuaded. Not staggering in the promises of God. Hope against hope. That's your destiny. That's your purpose. God's going to do it, and He's going to do it through you.

Regardless of what the flurry of crisis looks like, regardless of the attack on our religious liberties, the terrorist attacks, the opposition of the LGBT, we must refuse to be on the defensive but instead be on the offensive. We have to have hope. We have to be sure of our calling to take the kingdom of God to this world that is passing away. We must be committed to the prophetic charge that the kingdoms of this world shall become the kingdoms of our God and of His Christ.

Chapter Eight

What Are You Going to Do About It?

"Only ask, and I will give you the nations as your inheritance, the whole earth as your possession." – Psalm 2:8 (NLT)

In the last chapter, we considered the fifth way that Christians should respond in the plight of trials and crises: taking the gospel and preaching the gospel to the whole world and orchestrating massive evangelism across this earth! That's really what'll make the difference. No matter what we do it's ultimately still going to come down to Christians preaching truth.

The Lord is calling us to another place of confidence and boldness. He wants us to stand for Truth and preach a message that's full of hope. We must also preach a message that's full of faith—a message that clearly communicates that there's a light at the end of the tunnel—despite the chaos. We must lay a foundation of prayer that will later fuel our message of hope. Our prayers cannot be worried-filled prayers—*"Oh, God, what are we going do? It looks like disaster's coming! This is just the end! We're going to die!"* No, sir! Our faith is renewed! We always keep our faith alive because we know that faith is the substance of all things hoped for and the evidence of things not seen (Hebrews 11:1).

Nehemiah's Response to Crisis

The book of Nehemiah almost perfectly capsulizes and brings together a lot of what we've covered up to this point. It presents the classic Christian response to crisis! If you remember, Nehemiah was serving King Artaxerxes in Susa as his cupbearer, but then the word came to him:

> *"And they said unto me, The remnant that are left of the captivity there in the province are in great affliction and reproach: the wall of Jerusalem also is broken down, and the gates thereof are burned with fire.*
> *"And it came to pass, when I heard these words, that I sat down and wept, and mourned certain days, and fasted, and prayed before the God of heaven,*
> *"And said, I beseech thee, O LORD God of heaven, the great and terrible God, that keepeth covenant and mercy for them that love him and observe his commandments..."* – Nehemiah 1:3–5

Nehemiah Was Moved by What He Saw, and Then He Prayed

Nehemiah received the word that the remnant of captive Jews in the province was in great affliction. The wall of Jerusalem had been broken down, and the gates had been burned. Even though Nehemiah was working as a member of the king's staff, when he heard this awful news, he identified with his people, suffering beyond the luxury and comfort of the Shushan palace. He recognized that this was a problem, and it touched his heart. He immediately broke down and cried.

Now, let me ask you this: what situation or circumstance—other than your own personal circumstances—would break you if you received tragic news about that situation? What tragedy regarding someone else (beyond your family) would compel you to take action? If you heard about that person's plight, would you identify with it as if it were your own and take personal responsibility for it? Would you be unable to ignore it or disassociate yourself from their predicament? Would you recognize that this is something you have to address? Would you say, "I cannot just sit back and do nothing? I must be involved. I must make something happen!?"

Nehemiah understood that even though he was with the king and removed from the circumstances of this captivity, he identified with the Jews and was alarmed when he heard the walls were broken down.

When Nehemiah received the terrible news that the gates were burned with fire, he "sat down and wept, and mourned…" (Nehemiah 1:4). He fasted and prayed before the God of heaven. Before he made a move, he sought God.

His fasting was not to impress God or others. He wanted God's attention because he was broken. There are many reasons why we should fast, and the Scriptures teach that one of the reasons is for the sake of others. So, in this case, Nehemiah fasted on behalf of his people, the Jews:

> *"O Lord, God of heaven, the great and awesome God who keeps his covenant of unfailing love with those who love him and obey his commands, listen to my prayer! Look down and see me praying night and day for your people Israel. I confess that we have sinned against you. Yes, even my own family and I have sinned! We have sinned terribly by not obeying the commands, decrees, and regulations that you gave us through your servant Moses.*
>
> *Please remember what you told your servant Moses: 'If you are unfaithful to me, I will scatter you among the nations. But if you return to me and obey my commands and live by them, then even if you are exiled to the ends of the earth, I will bring you back to the place I have chosen for my name to be honored.'"*

We also have to look at our current lives and times and the situations we're facing in America right now. Talk about walls being broken down! We're so vulnerable right now! When I say "we" though, "we" could apply to any people. It could be a people by culture. It could be a people by race. It could be a people nationally. We're in a place where we are susceptible to the enemy wreaking havoc on us. Because the walls of protection are not up, we have been left exposed to the enemy's attack which brings havoc and destruction.

We must recognize how important it is as intercessors to build these walls! But we must be intentional and volitional in our response. Take note of what Nehemiah did. He sought the Lord first (Nehemiah 1:5).

Nehemiah Took Ownership for the Devastation

Secondly, Nehemiah identified with the sin of his people. In Nehemiah 1:6, he said, *"...confess the sins of the children of Israel, which <u>we</u> have sinned against thee...."* He owned the sin of his people. Interestingly enough, Moses did this, and Daniel did this when God's people turned their backs on God. Verse 6 also records Nehemiah confessing, *"...both I and my father's house have sinned."*

> *"We have dealt very corruptly against thee, and have not kept the commandments, nor the statutes, nor the judgments, which thou commandedst thy servant Moses. Remember, I beseech thee, the word that thou commandedst thy servant Moses, saying, If ye transgress, I will scatter you abroad among the nations...."* – Nehemiah 1:7–8

Nehemiah Asked for Mercy from a Sovereign God

Nehemiah recognized that God was in control of this situation, but he could not come to the Lord out of a place of brashness and say, "Well, God, how could you allow this to happen?"

As Christians, sometimes we get this thing confused, and we think God owes us something. We demand from Him, saying, "Well, God, You promised us this. We're Your chosen people, so how could You allow this to happen?" No!

First, you go to the Lord in brokenness because what we deserve is death. There is nothing in life that we can say we deserve from God because the wages of sin is death. We all fail miserably before Him, so there's no place left for pride.

Even if you're in a position to step in for another person and try to rebuild a wall on somebody else's behalf, you better get things right with God first. Acknowledge on everyone's behalf that we're in a place of vulnerability, and we need God's mercy.

Nehemiah goes on in verse 11:

> *"O LORD, I beseech thee, let now thine ear be attentive to the prayer of thy servant, and to the prayer of thy servants, who*

desire to fear thy name: and prosper, I pray thee, thy servant this day, and grant him mercy in the sight of this man. For I was the king's cupbearer."

Nehemiah Asked for Favor from Ruling Men

First, Nehemiah asked for mercy from God. Secondly, he asked for favor from man.

"Then the king said unto me, For what dost thou make request? So I prayed to the God of heaven. And I said unto the king, If it please the king, and if thy servant have found favour in thy sight, that thou wouldest send me unto Judah, unto the city of my fathers' sepulchres, that I may build it."
— Nehemiah 2:4–5

It's important to have a good reputation before men. At this point, if Nehemiah had not faithfully stewarded all the responsibilities that the king had entrusted to him, he would not have been in a position to approach the king and ask the king to bless him and release him to go help his people.

Nehemiah's response to his people's crisis proceeded in this order: First, he went to God (Nehemiah 2:4)—the King of kings and the Lord of lords—and asked the Lord for favor with the king of Susa. Second, Nehemiah petitioned the king, *"...send me unto Judah, unto the city of my fathers' sepulchres, that I may rebuild it" (Nehemiah 2:5b).*

Nehemiah 2:6 says, *"So it pleased the king to send me; and I set him a time."* In verse 7, he continued, *"Moreover I said unto the king, If it please the king, let letters be given me to the governors beyond the river, that they may convey me over till I come into Judah...."*

Nehemiah wanted not just letters but letters of favor and approval as he went through so that he could get the materials he needed to build this wall. Nehemiah was expecting favor all the way around. Imagine Nehemiah approaching King Artaxerxes and saying, "King, please give me a letter asking various officials along the way to give me the resources I need to go build this wall." Nehemiah was determined to build the wall, but he didn't have the resources. But these ungodly Gentiles had the resources that he needed, and he wasn't afraid to ask for them.

Understand this: we should expect favor. If there's work to be done, we must expect that the resources are there.

Now, here's a profound declaration that defies political correctness: the wealth of the Gentiles has purposefulness. They don't know what to do with it. It's for their own advantage and their greed. They are holding what belongs to us because we can give purpose for money. I don't know why, but sometimes, God allows them to be stewards over great wealth. But that wealth is going to be used for the devil's purposes unless God can get to them and ask them to hand over the possessions, He's given them—just like Jesus said, "you will see a young donkey tied there that no one has ever ridden. Untie it and bring it here. If anyone asks, 'What are you doing?' just say, 'The Lord needs it'" (Mark 11:2-3). We too can say, "Empty your bank account. The Lord has need of it. Just give me a million dollars to do the work." When you do put yourself in that position, you have to be convinced that this is God—so convinced that you don't even understand "no." "No" is not even an option.

A lot of times, we lose out because we are too timid with our requests. We have to recognize that we can request it in faith— nothing wavering and with no doubt in our minds. Nehemiah was going before kings, so even though he had a letter of endorsement from his king, he still had to convince other kings and governing officials that this was what he needed to get the job done.

Many times, we are intimidated by other folks' wealth. We're intimidated by their posture. We're intimidated by their authority. We're intimidated by the role they play. Why be intimidated? They're just people. They have the same frailties in the body as you, so even if they've been blessed with worldly wealth and possessions, they still have to answer to God the same way we do. So, don't have any intimidation about asking because if *you're* convinced this is God, you can convince them, and they're going to believe it when you boldly explain your vision. Nehemiah did that very thing. He said, "let me have letters," (Nehemiah 2:7) and he received those letters and went on his way.

Nehemiah Experienced Opposition

Now, of course, you know some enemies were opposing the rebuilding. In everything we do—if it's worth anything—there will always be enemies who will come against it. Sometimes, we think the Lord is just going to clear all of the enemies out of the way. We assume no one is going to talk about us; nobody's going to misunderstand us; everybody's going to conclude that we're doing the right thing. But if you receive any mandate from God, there will be enemies who will work against what you're doing. Expect that. The fact that it is from God should alert you that there will be enemies.

In the New Living Translation of Nehemiah 4:1–2a, it says this:

"Sanballat was very angry when he learned that we were rebuilding the wall. He flew into a rage and mocked the Jews, saying in front of his friends and the Samarian army officers, 'What does this bunch of poor, feeble Jews think they're doing? Do they think they can build the wall in a single day by just offering a few sacrifices?'"

Sanballat was protesting, "You think you're just going to pray and fast, and then you're going to accomplish some great task?"

"Tobiah the Ammonite, who was standing beside him, remarked, "That stone wall would collapse if even a fox walked along the top of it!" (Nehemiah 4:3, NLT).

Nehemiah's critics thought his plan was the most ridiculous thing they had ever heard. "How are they going to build a wall? It's not going to happen! As a matter of fact, that wall's so weak that the whole thing would go down if a fox goes across it!" So, they're prophesying doom against this wall.

Remember that the wall had been broken down, and the gates had been burned. So, how in the world can you bring life from something that's dead? It's too charred, and the rubble is too much. The wall has been burned to the ground.

People today ask the same thing about the possibility of a spiritual revival. They ask, "How are you going to revive dead bones? These bones are dry. These bones are empty. These bones have no life at all. How in the world do you think you're going to revive these dead bones?" This is the kind of opposition and skepticism Nehemiah was facing.

When you're doing something for God that's different than what people are used to, their reaction will be negative—because people don't know what to do with things that are a little different. The first reaction is, "Aww man, how could that happen? That's never been done before." Not only were Nehemiah's critics predicting the impossibility of the wall being rebuilt, but they were also pronouncing that it would be a public shame.

What we learn from Nehemiah's example is if we've been praying and seeking God for something, and if God has determined that something will come to pass—if God's hand is on it—then our expectation should be that God's going to build a strong wall. He's going to do something incredible in the midst of devastation.

What was Nehemiah's response? He prayed:

"Hear us, our God, for we are being mocked. May their scoffing fall back on their own heads, and may they themselves become captives in a foreign land! Do not ignore their guilt. Do not blot out their sins, for they have provoked you to anger here in front of the builders." – Nehemiah 4:4 (NLT)

In other words, Nehemiah was praying, "Lord, take 'em out!" There's a time to pray for mercy for your enemies, but in *this* case, Nehemiah said, "Hold on! Time out! If they're going to take this kind of position against us, then, God, deal with them!" In this case, he said, "Don't forget their sin. *Don't* blot it out because they're making a public spectacle of us"— ultimately mocking God. And the Bible declares in Galatians 6:7 (AMP), *"Do not be deceived, God is not mocked."*

God does deal with the enemies of the Jews seriously, even though He may use Israel's enemies to deal with their sins and bring them under some kind of judgment—which was the case with Judah's captivity in Susa. Any country or nation that is used against Israel already has some kind of judgment against it just by the fact that it was willing to oppose God's people. As an "enemy agent" against captive Israel, Susa was opposing God's people. God is predisposed to fight against those who fight against His people. Therefore, He will hear a prayer like Nehemiah's prayer.

Nehemiah Worked Wholeheartedly

Nehemiah 4:6 (NLT) says, *"At last the wall was completed to half its height around the entire city, for the people had worked with enthusiasm."* The New King James Version says, *"...the people had a mind to work."* God had given them an empowerment of His Spirit and a willingness to work.

For Christians today, every substantial work in God's kingdom is going to require something of us. Working for the Lord is going to be sacrificial work.

Along with prayer, there has to be some kind of action. The Bible says that faith without works is dead (James 2:26). We may say that we're in faith, and we say that we're believing God for something to happen, but if we do nothing, then nothing can happen.

Now, in walks the opposition:

"But when Sanballat and Tobiah and the Arabs, Ammonites, and Ashdodites heard that the work was going ahead and that the gaps in the wall of Jerusalem were being repaired, they were furious. They all made plans to come and fight against Jerusalem and throw us into confusion. But we prayed to our God and guarded the city day and night to protect ourselves." – Nehemiah 4:7–8 (NLT)

"Nevertheless we made our prayer unto our God, and set a watch against them day and night, because of them." – Nehemiah 4:9

The Bible says you must watch and pray. You have to man your post. You can't just sit back and pretend your enemy's not there. No, even when you're doing the work, somebody has to watch your back. You have to watch out for the enemy because he will try to come against you. The wonderful lesson from Nehemiah is even though the enemy showed up, that did not stop God's people from doing what they were called to do.

Nehemiah Encountered Fatigue

The workers didn't remain resolute forever though. In verse 10 (NLT), Nehemiah recounted, *"Then the people of Judah began to complain, 'The workers are getting tired, and there is so much rubble to be moved. We will never be able to build the wall by ourselves.'"*

The workers gave in to a spirit of negativity, to a lack of faith, and unbelief. They began to complain among themselves and to the authorities, "We will never get this done!"

With any great work, there is always that point where it looks like you're fighting against a brick wall. You begin to wonder, "Is this thing really worth it? Can I really succeed? Is it really worth the effort to try to make this happen when it might be doomed to fail? After all, I'm tired!" However, the Lord is faithful. He does rebuild your strength. Angels rebuild your strength. There is a time for the rebuilding of strength.

But there is also a time when you have to dig in. You just can't stop in the middle of a major task like this and say, "I'm tired." Once you give in to fatigue, you begin to believe it won't happen. That's what the people of Judah said: *"We will never be able to rebuild the wall by ourselves" (Nehemiah 4:10b, NLT)*. That's when the enemy moves in for the kill: *"Meanwhile, our enemies were saying, 'Before they know what's happening, we will swoop down on them and kill them and end their work'" (Nehemiah 4:11, NLT)*.

The enemy said, "Aha! We got 'em right where we want them. Now's the time to come in and take 'em out!" The adversary, the devil, is always working against the people of God. With fatigue weighing down their resolve, they moved into a vulnerable position. The enemy is cunning. When the workers were tired of building the wall and susceptible to discouragement, doubt, and unbelief, that's when their enemy said they were going to swoop down.

God's people opened the door to the enemy's attack through murmuring and complaining. And so the devil said, "Great! That's just where I want you to be. I've been waiting for this moment because I knew you guys couldn't stay together. So, I'm going to swoop down while you're still complaining and unfocused. I'm coming in, and I'm going to take you out!"

The Bible tells you not to be ignorant of the devil's devices. He's not that smart, but his strategies are always operating against us.

> *"The Jews who lived near the enemy came and told us again and again, 'They will come from all directions and attack us!' So I placed armed guards behind the lowest parts of the wall in the exposed areas. I stationed the people to stand guard by families, armed with swords, spears, and bows. Then as I looked over the situation, I called together the nobles and the rest of the people and said to them, 'Don't be afraid of the enemy! Remember the Lord, who is great and glorious, and fight for your brothers, your sons, your daughters, your wives, and your homes!'" – Nehemiah 4:12–14 (NLT)*

Nehemiah Encouraged Unity

It's so important to have family unity. And I don't just mean with those who are biologically related to you. Jesus said, those who do the will of God are My mother and brother and My family (Mark 34:35). In other words, my true family and your true family are the ones following God.

With all of the relational upheaval in our communities— shootings, protests, police brutality—this spiritual truth is more important now than ever before. Even though there's an allegiance based on natural blood relations, it should not supersede the spiritual blood relationship that we share as believers in the Lord Jesus Christ.

Across all levels of social media, we hear discussions about racial healing and advocating that all those who are white or all those who are black or Hispanic need to stick together based on race. No, no, no. It doesn't matter what your blood or tribe is. If you are a believer in Christ, your true family is the family of God. There is no substitute for this. Jesus said that the ones who hear God's word and obey it are His family (Luke 8:21).

Natural families are called to protect each other and fight any enemy who would seek to destroy the family. Likewise, the body of Christ—God's family—must unify and fight our adversary, the devil, when he attacks the Church. When God's people are tired and not unified, the enemy gains access to work against us. We cannot simply identify ourselves as individuals who have been brought together in the church—a group of individuals, or a group of attendees, or a group of members. What God sees is one body—that we are

of one blood. We've been bought with the same price: His blood. We are a true family.

Nehemiah Fought Back

Nehemiah said, "Don't be afraid of the enemy. Fight as you've never fought! Fight for your sons and daughters because we're in this thing together."

Don't be afraid of the enemy. Don't let fear overtake you. The devil loves it when you disqualify yourself from winning the battle due to fear. He comes like a roaring lion, seeking whom he may devour (1 Peter 5:8). Usually, he "brings the big guns out" to intimidate you into believing you're not going to make it—whether it's building the wall in Jerusalem or fighting present-day evil in our land.

Your adversary, the devil, wants you to believe you can never win. He wants us to be convinced that the evil is so great, the perversion is so rampant, the laws are so unjust, and the drug war is so uncontrollable, why even try to fight the enemy? How in the world can we face these giants? Even though it seems as though we can never win, fight for your family! That was Nehemiah's admonition to his generation: Remember the Lord thy God and fight for your brothers and your sons and daughters and your wives and your homes

(Nehemiah 4:14). A family is more victorious as one unit than one individual fighting alone.

> *"When our enemies heard that we knew of their plans and that God had frustrated them, we all returned to our work on the wall. But from then on, only half my men worked while the other half stood guard with spears, shields, bows, and coats of mail." – Nehemiah 4:15–16a (NLT)*

This is the side of God and His people where God is not only merciful and loving but also awesome and mighty in battle! People tend to think that Jesus is a nonviolent God. He would never hurt anybody. He's so sweet. He's sweet, I know, but Jesus is not playing. He's coming back with a sword.

The people of Judah were manning their posts, armed with spears, swords, and shields, while the work on the wall continued! The post that God gives you is all a part of a purpose in your life. Sure, there are always things that are going to cause you to question whether it's worth it, whether you should do it, whether you can maintain it, and whether it's worth your time. The devil wants you to tuck your tail and run.

But the Lord says, when I return, I'm coming to see if I can find faith on the earth (Luke 18:8). Without faith, it's impossible to please Him. He's not ever going to be pleased with your leaving your post and running. No matter what the situation is, stand your ground before the enemy. Fight to the end.

In Nehemiah 4:16b–17 (NLT), it says, *"The leaders stationed themselves behind the people of Judah who were building the wall. The laborers carried on their work with one hand supporting their load and one hand holding a weapon."* I love the visual of that! In reality, we're never supposed to stop fighting. We must always be prepared for war. Christians aren't called to a life free from problems and opposition. Just ask Paul about that. Ask Jesus what He went through. Some of Christ's apostles were put on a cross, turned upside down, and killed just to mock the cross. John was beheaded. These weren't easy deaths.

What I'm saying to you is this: We have a strength inside of us that empowers us to fight. We're fighters. We're not going to back down to the enemy! We fight the enemy spiritually, but we don't spend all our time fighting folks in the flesh! God's made you a fighter to fight against spiritual wickedness in high places.

The devil will try to pull you into this disharmony, discord, and criticism, but it pulls you off the things of God! You need to fight against the forces of evil—not fighting somebody's flesh! Most of the time, it won't do any good anyway. You have to see the bigger picture here and use your time and focus on what God's called you to do!

We are fighters—spiritual fighters. We will wrestle. That's why we have to be spiritually strong because it takes so much effort to regain your strength once you lose it. That's why we have to know the Word. That's why we have to pray. That's why we have to stay committed and stay in communion with the Lord. That's why it's so important to stay close to the fire.

The children of Israel were promised they were going to have a land of milk and honey, but they were going to have to fight some enemies to get it. There were giants there, possessing that land. Israel had to go in and tell them, "Get off my land."

God says in Psalm 2:8a, *"Ask of me, and I shall give thee the heathen for thine inheritance...."* In the midst of world crises, political turmoil and social unrest, there are unreached people who need to hear the gospel. In crisis, the people of God must preach the gospel and conquer the world. But you will have to spiritually fight some giants to conquer the world. Don't back down. Get as close as you can to build your strength up.

Nehemiah 4:18–20 (NLT) says this:

"All the builders had a sword belted to their side. The trumpeter stayed with me to sound the alarm. Then I explained to the nobles and officials and all the people, 'The work is very spread out, and we are widely separated from each other along the wall. When you hear the blast of the trumpet, rush to wherever it is sounding. Then our God will fight for us!'"

Many times, in doing the work God has called us to, we might be spread out because we have different responsibilities. But our strength comes from being together. So, when the alarm sounded and the trumpet was blown, the workers were instructed to come together, and then the Lord would fight for them. The mandate was *not* "spread out and become isolated!" No, no. It's in unity and togetherness that the Lord will fight for us! There's something about the power of standing strong together—in that time, you watch and see what my God will do. We won't even have to fight in that battle. When it gets down to it, the Lord has to fight it anyway.

After coming together, remain on guard at all times.

> *"During this time, none of us—not I, nor my relatives, nor my servants, nor the guards who were with me—ever took off our clothes. We carried our weapons with us at all times, even when we went for water." – Nehemiah 4:23 (NLT)*

Stay on guard. Don't ever, ever drop your weapon. For the time that we're living in, we cannot afford it. Don't be surprised when there's a Sanballat or Tobiah or Ammonites opposing you. Actually, you should expect it. But be convinced that no weapon formed against you shall prosper. The Bible reveals that in the end, we win. Let this be your personal testimony. Let it be the testimony of your church. Let that be the testimony of the body of Christ. That even in this time, God is fighting our battles, but we're ready, we're armed, and we're packing!

Chapter Nine

A Change of Heart

"His love has the first and last word in everything we do." –
2 Corinthians 5:13 (MSG)

Back in the Day

Before I became a Christian, I saw everything in the context of race. I was born and raised in Atlanta, Georgia, during the end of the racial segregation era and in the midst of the Civil Rights Movement.

My father was a postal worker, and my mother was a teacher. So, our family was doing well socio-economically for black folks during that era. Our family lived in a segregated, black neighborhood. I went to a racially segregated, all-black nursery school, an all-black elementary school, and a black high school.

I was intent to have the finest education among those who were considered to be the nation's "black intelligentsia," so I chose to go to college at Howard University—a historically black college. Even though I was accepted at several reputable, predominantly white universities, I intentionally chose to throw my cap in the company of black collegiate leaders.

I chose to attend Howard University not only because of its status among the black intelligentsia but also because of its location—in the heart of Washington, DC, a predominantly black city—affectionately named by black folks as "The Chocolate City." Washington, DC, was where the "Who's Who" of black life in America lived, governed, entertained, and made things happen. I was deliberate in choosing The Chocolate City. It was the hub of decision-making, as the capital city of our nation and the hub of black activity.

Back then, in the late 1970s and early '80s, student leaders glorified the militancy of the '60s. We were willing to protest anything and everything. I remember storming the Administration Building of Howard University, along with scores of my peers, in protest of the university's stance on our student activities and school policies. We took over the building for the cause of students' rights and academic freedom! We also protested in the streets of Washington, DC, over the controversy and racial tensions surrounding the Wilmington Ten—a famously coined reference to ten civil rights activists who had been falsely accused and unwarrantedly imprisoned following a school desegregation boycott in Wilmington, North Carolina.

With my black card in one hand and my other hand raised in the "black power fist," I also marched on the National Mall in support of Martin Luther King's birthday becoming a national holiday. Stevie Wonder was there singing! I was there marching!

I was militant. I was involved in student government on Howard's campus and led the National Organization of Black University and College Students.

Because I was involved in student government right at the hub of black activity, I met the nation's most celebrated black leaders at that time: Nation of Islam leader Louis Farrakhan, California Congressman Ron Dellums, Rainbow PUSH Coalition founder Jessie Jackson, and civil rights activist Stokely Carmichael. I even knew Ron Karenga, the founder of the black holiday Kwanzaa.

Upon graduation, I pursued my law degree at Howard University as well. I had my black card. I was a born-and-bred, black-college-educated, more-power-to-the-people, burgeoning leader in my community. I was all about my blackness!

My entire life from infancy to young adulthood was steeped in blackness—completely engulfed in ethnocentric philosophy, an ethnocentric environment, and an ethnocentric value system.

A Transformative Love for God

"Because of all that God has done, we now have a new perspective. We used to show regard for people based on worldly standards and interests. No longer." – 2 Corinthians 5:16a (VOICE)

Although I was raised in the church, I began to make lifestyle choices in college that were antithetical to the teachings of Scripture—and I knew it. I would go out on weekends and get high, go to clubs, and so on.

One day, I had an encounter with God—all alone in my dorm room—recognizing that I was a sinner and that I had not fully surrendered the choices and direction of my life to Jesus Christ. Once I made a decision to follow Christ, my spirit was renewed, but my mind had not yet been renewed.

Even though I gave my life to the Lord, I did it in the context of race. My family experiences, my social experiences, and my academic career were mainly black. And it was in the midst of this consistently black existence that I met Jesus Christ. So, in a lock-step fashion, I exclusively sought out Bible teachers and Christian fellowship with people who were of the same race as me. But eventually, my zeal for God began to eclipse my racial preferences. God was transforming me—not only my spirit but also my soul (my mind, will, and emotional outlook on life).

One pivotal moment that changed all of that for me occurred at a meeting in the law school building of Howard University (a few years after my conversion encounter with God) when the Holy Spirit baptized me with His presence and power. My hunger for the Word of God was so consuming that I began to listen to Bible teachers whom I would have never listened to before because they were outside of my cultural experience and comfort zone.

Eventually, God began to deal with me about my priorities and vantage point in life. I had a driving passion for the causes of my people, but I began to wonder if that was all there was. My militancy still left something more to be desired.

It became apparent to me that my hunger and enthusiasm for God needed to precede my enthusiasm for my race...and that's exactly what happened! The cause of Christ became the controlling force in my life, instead of the causes promoting blackness. My hunger for the Bible was so consuming that it began to change my approach to life and overshadow everything I thought—without any realization on my part because it happened over time.

I realized that I had a deeply ingrained black state of thinking. And a key step in my spiritual growth, after receiving a renewed heart as a born-again Christian, was developing a correspondingly renewed mind—a state of thinking that became transformed by God's Word and *His way* of seeing things.

My understanding of the following Scripture brought my philosophical and cultural transformation to light:

> *"For the love of Christ constraineth us; because we thus judge, that if one died for all, then were all dead: And that he died for all, that THEY WHICH LIVE SHOULD NOT HENCEFORTH LIVE UNTO THEMSELVES, but unto him which died for them, and rose again. Wherefore henceforth KNOW WE NO MAN AFTER THE FLESH: yea, though we have known Christ after the flesh, yet now henceforth know we him no more. Therefore if any man be in Christ, he is a new creature: old things are passed away; behold, all things are become new."* – 2 Corinthians 5:14–17 (KJV, emphasis mine)

My "race-replacement moment" occurred when I recognized that my new love for Jesus Christ compelled me to no longer "live unto myself." I had become "a new creature," a spiritually new being. The old motivations that were ruling my life had passed away.

Verses 16 and 17 are crucial to understanding the transformation that takes place once a person is "in Christ." When the Bible refers to our "flesh," it's referring to the emotional, physiological, and moral state of humanity, which relates to everything through the five senses and adheres to the standards of the temporary physical world.

Once our lives have been translated from "the flesh" and "into Christ" (the new spiritual state of every believer in Jesus Christ), we should no longer live to accommodate ourselves and cater to our flesh (our appetites and preferences) or our race because it's a part of our original physiological being. We're now meant to live for something much bigger than ourselves.

In 2 Corinthians 5, the Apostle Paul explains that once this spiritual awakening takes place in a Christian's heart, not only our eternal destiny changes but also our motivations and perspectives will change *"that they which live should not henceforth live unto themselves"* (2 Corinthians 5:15). Our purpose changes. Jesus Christ died for us so that we would live—not for ourselves—but for Him who died and rose from the dead.

God brought me into a totally different understanding of why I was born. My goal was to no longer live on this earth, endeavoring to please myself. The Apostle Paul's declaration, *"wherefore henceforth know we no man after the flesh"* (2 Corinthians 5:16a), suggests that we're to no longer selfishly evaluate others primarily from the human standards of this temporary, physical world.

A few different translations explain 2 Corinthians 5:16a this way:

- VOICE: *"We used to show regard for people based on worldly standards and interests."*
- NLT: *"We have stopped evaluating others from a human point of view."*
- PHILLIPS: *"This means that our knowledge of men can no longer be based on their outward lives."*

There's a greater purpose for us to be here. Our cause should no longer be a self-serving cause. Our new lives in Christ become ones marked by dedicated service.

This new understanding became the first in a chain of events in my life in which Christ's love became the first and last word in everything I did (2 Corinthians 5:13). The Lord had not only reconciled me to Him but had also begun to change my orientation and value system toward those outside my race.

Vertical Reconciliation

Before you can fully understand racial reconciliation, you must first understand *the vertical element* of reconciliation. You might be familiar with the traditional King James Version of the Apostle Paul's description of vertical reconciliation:

"And all things are of God, who hath reconciled us to himself by Jesus Christ, and hath given to us THE MINISTRY OF RECONCILIATION; To wit, that God was in Christ, reconciling the world unto himself, not imputing their trespasses unto them; and hath committed unto us the word of reconciliation. Now then we are ambassadors for Christ, as though God did beseech you by us: we pray you in Christ's stead, be ye reconciled to God." – 2 Corinthians 5:18–20 (Emphasis mine)

A paraphrase describing this inward, spiritual reconciliation explains it this way:

"Now we look inside, and what we see is that anyone united with the Messiah GETS A FRESH START, IS CREATED NEW. The old life is gone; a new life burgeons! Look at it! All this comes from THE GOD WHO SETTLED THE RELATIONSHIP BETWEEN US AND HIM, AND THEN CALLED US TO SETTLE OUR RELATIONSHIPS WITH EACH OTHER. GOD PUT THE WORLD SQUARE WITH HIMSELF THROUGH THE MESSIAH, GIVING THE WORLD A FRESH START BY OFFERING FORGIVENESS OF SINS. God has given us the task of telling everyone what he is doing. We're Christ's representatives. God uses us to persuade men and women to drop their differences and enter into God's work of making things right between them. We're speaking for Christ himself now: Become friends with God.... How? you ask. In Christ. God put the wrong on him who never did anything wrong, so we could be put right with God." – 2 Corinthians 5:17–21 (MSG, emphasis mine)

From 2 Corinthians 5:20, we learn that God is *first* reconciling the world to Himself. God always calls us to vertical reconciliation *first*! Anyone desiring to approach God must come to the Father through the Son. *"God put the world square with Himself through the*

Messiah, giving the world a fresh start by offering forgiveness of sins."

The pattern you'll see in Scripture is that the early Christians appealed to people to "get right with God" or "be reconciled to God," prioritizing that man's primary and biggest problem is his sin debt and a relational problem with a holy God to whom he must be reconciled for breaking fellowship with Him. *"We beg you, as though Christ Himself were here pleading with you, receive the love He offers you— be reconciled to God."*

If you haven't been reconciled unto God, then you judge everything "by the flesh" or from a human perspective because that's all you know. "The flesh" is our soul's condition before it is influenced and governed by God. A judgment "by the flesh" is a perspective or a state of a mind that has not yet been renewed by the Holy Spirit and the Word of God.

> *"For who could really understand a man's inmost thoughts except the spirit of the man himself? How much less could anyone understand the thoughts of God except the very Spirit of God? And the marvelous thing is this, that we now receive not the spirit of the world BUT THE SPIRIT OF GOD HIMSELF, SO THAT WE CAN ACTUALLY UNDERSTAND something of God's generosity toward us....*
>
> *"BUT THE UNSPIRITUAL MAN SIMPLY CANNOT ACCEPT THE MATTERS WHICH THE SPIRIT DEALS WITH—THEY JUST DON'T MAKE SENSE TO HIM, FOR, AFTER ALL, YOU MUST BE SPIRITUAL TO SEE SPIRITUAL THINGS. THE SPIRITUAL MAN, ON THE OTHER HAND, HAS AN INSIGHT INTO THE MEANING OF EVERYTHING, though his insight may baffle the man of the world. This is because the former is SHARING IN GOD'S WISDOM, and 'Who has known the mind of the Lord that he may instruct him?' Incredible as it may sound, we who are spiritual have the very thoughts of Christ!"* – 1 Corinthians 2:10b–12, 14–16 (PHILLIPS, emphasis mine)

A person can only conclude things about life by what he knows and by the limited experiences he understands. In order to conclude things based on God's perspective, a person would need to have the Spirit of God influencing and informing his or her mind. Why? Because fallen man doesn't think the same as God does nor see life the way that God does.

> *"For My thoughts are not your thoughts, Nor are your ways My ways," declares the LORD. 'For as the heavens are higher than the earth, So are My ways higher than your ways and My thoughts than your thoughts.'" – Isaiah 55:8–9 (NASB)*

Horizontal Reconciliation

Once you have been reconciled to God—which is the vertical reconciliation you experience at conversion—then God wants you to share the good news of your reconciliation with others and invite them into that peace with God. So, your first assignment (once you've given your life to Christ) is preaching Jesus, teaching Jesus, and being an example of Jesus in this world. It's your mandate.

Remember Paul's explanation to the church at Corinth:

> *"...for he has reconciled us to himself through Jesus Christ; and he has made us agents of the reconciliation. God was in Christ personally reconciling the world to himself—not counting their sins against them—and has commissioned us with the message of reconciliation. We are now Christ's ambassadors, as though God were appealing direct to you through us. As his personal representatives we say, 'Make your peace with God.'" – 2 Corinthians 5:18–21a (PHILLIPS)*

What a privilege! God has made us agents of reconciliation—His representatives—and He *commissioned us* with the message of reconciliation! As believers in Jesus Christ and His ambassadors, we are called to be reconciled not only to God but also to our brother—

that's the horizontal reconciliation mandated by God in 2 Corinthians 5.

> *"God has given us the task of telling everyone what he is doing. We're Christ's representatives. God uses us to persuade men and women to drop their differences and enter into God's work of making things right between them. We're speaking for Christ himself now" (2 Corinthians 5:20 MSG).*

The ministry of reconciliation is the task of telling everyone that God is about the business of reconciling mankind (who is separated from God) back to Himself. It's the task God has assigned to us. *"God uses us to persuade men and women to drop their differences and enter into God's work of making things right between them"* (2 Corinthians 5:20 MSG).

This is such a delicate and crucial task here—especially as our brothers and sisters of other races need to drop their grievances and enter into a reconciled relationship with each other. After all, most relational conflicts stem from a vertical disconnection with God first, then—out of the broken vertical relationship with God—the horizontal relationships between brothers and neighbors break down. As a minister of racial reconciliation, we're entering into God's work of making things right between the races.

Paul said, *"We're speaking for Christ Himself now" (2 Corinthians 5:20 MSG).* So, as Christ's representatives, we have to be careful of what we say to one another during a painful time of racial tension and crisis. God is requiring us to speak the truth in love at that moment. We are His ambassadors sent on assignment to address the recent issues relating to racial conflict and cultural divisiveness in America.

As Christians, we can be tempted to brush the problem with racial conflict and cultural divisiveness under the rug because it's too controversial. There are also many Christians who don't accept the assignment as ambassadors of reconciliation because they see black Christians or white Christians as their enemy. Yet Paul made it clear in his letter to the church in Galatia that all Christians belong to the same family, sired by our Heavenly Father, Jehovah Rapha—the Lord who heals us.

> *"All of you are God's children because of your faith in Christ Jesus. And when you were baptized, it was as though you had put on Christ in the same way you put on new clothes. Faith in Christ Jesus is what makes each of you equal with each other, whether you are a Jew or a Greek, a slave or a free person, a man or a woman. So if you belong to Christ, you are now part of Abraham's family, and you will be given what God has promised." – Galatians 3:26–29 (CEV)*

When we speak the truth to our brother about reconciling the racial conflicts so prevalent today, we must address a sober spiritual irony that the media is overlooking in the Black Lives Matter controversy. Blacks are demanding justice, yet the black looters and rioters and murderers who are retaliating in the streets are violating the practices and principles that ensure justice!

According to Isaiah 59, a nation that has rejected the laws and ways of God cannot expect God to show up on the scene, fix the problem, and give them justice. The prophet Isaiah makes it plain:

> *"Listen! The LORD's arm is not too weak to save you, nor is his ear too deaf to hear you call. It's your sins that have cut you off from God. Because of your sins, he has turned away and will not listen anymore." – Isaiah 59:1–2 (NLT)*

The people can march in the streets all day long, demanding justice, but they're not going to receive justice. Why? Because the ones who are instigating the wrongful acts in our communities will be wronged in return. Is just desserts for their own behavior. It's a spiritual condition decreed by the Almighty God: where sin abounds and the depraved hearts of man rebel against God, God's ear will be deaf to their cries. The Bible says that as long as man is evil, his evil heart will judge all situations with evil motives and see everything through the lens of evil (Titus 1:15).

As ministers or agents of reconciliation, who analyze the events of our world through the spiritual perspective of God's Word, we can offer valid solutions to the racial conflicts we're facing. When you understand God's Word, you understand what's happening *beneath the surface* of the racial and political unrest.

When and how can justice be experienced in our national race crisis? When we acknowledge our wrongdoing, cry out for God's mercy, and turn back to God. Then the issues that lay at the foundation of racial division will be forgiven. Then God will move on behalf of those crying out for His help. The same repentance it takes to be reconciled vertically to God is also the repentance necessary to horizontally reconcile the races.

As we observe the racial tensions brewing and erupting across the country, we Christians—with a renewed mind and renewed purpose—must not react the same way non-Christians do. We must not "judge after the flesh" (John 8:15) when we analyze the controversies behind the police shootings. We must not cry, "An eye for an eye and a tooth for a tooth" (Exodus 21:24)! We must have a different spirit—a son of Issachar spirit that can discern the times.

It is true that the criminal justice system is far from being just. But when you know your Bible, you can discern the issues brimming beneath the surface of the criminal justice system.

In Proverbs 14:34 (GNT), King Solomon addressed the effects of piety or rebellion on the peace and welfare of a community: *"Righteousness makes a nation great; sin is a disgrace to any nation."*

Paul wrote to the church in Rome concerning the sinfulness of man:

> *"...all people, whether Jews or Gentiles, are under the power of sin. As the Scriptures say, 'No one is righteous— not even one...no one is seeking God." – Romans 3:9b–11 (NLT)*
>> *"For everyone has sinned; we all fall short of God's glorious standard." – Romans 3:23 (NLT)*

When you understand what the Bible has to say about the sinfulness of man and how righteousness exalts a nation, you have the spiritual wisdom to make sense out of the racially charged problems at the center of the Black Lives Matter Movement: prisons overcrowded with black youths, disproportionate arrests, and arraignments for black youths, wrongful deaths, and police brutality among black youths.

No matter which side you take in the Black Lives Matter controversy, there is a biblical explanation for the conflict and a biblical solution to the crisis. All of the mayhem and retaliation stirred up by race rioters and the bias in our criminal justice system can both be summed up with Isaiah's commentary:

> *"Your hands are the hands of murderers, and your fingers are filthy with sin. Your lips are full of lies, and your mouth spews corruption. No one cares about being fair and honest. The people's lawsuits are based on lies.*
>
> *"They conceive evil deeds and then give birth to sin.... All their activity is filled with sin, and violence is their trademark.*
>
> *"Their feet run to do evil, and they rush to commit murder. They think only about sinning.... They don't know where to find peace or what it means to be just and good.... So there is no justice among us, and we know nothing about right living." – Isaiah 59:3–4, 6–9 (NLT)*

The Paradox of Justice and Racial Disparity

> *"The Ten Commandments have had a significant impact on the development of secular legal codes of the Western World...Religion has been closely identified with our history and government." – Chief Justice William Rehnquist*[9]

---

[9] Jay Alan Sekulow, <u>Foundations of Freedom</u>, page 53. American Center for Law and Justice, Washington, D.C.

We're all familiar with the images or statues of the scales of justice. The scales are weighted evenly to demonstrate that the law will be fair and balanced. Justice requires that the penalty paid or the punishment given should be congruent with the crime that was committed. *Injustice occurs when the punishment meted out is far too severe or not commensurate to the weight of the offense.*

Unfortunately, there is a great disparity of punishment-to-crime ratios among blacks. Too often the "time doesn't match the crime." Blacks are exploited or trapped within the legal system. This tragedy falls short of the Constitution's goal to "provide for the common defense, promote the general welfare, and secure the blessings of liberty to ourselves and our posterity."[10]

When we hear cries for justice regarding the recent legal cases in the news, what people are really questioning is the <u>balance of those weights</u> holding the incident of the crime on one side and the appropriate penalty for the crime on the other side.

Our nation's judges are mandated to weigh both sides—offense and penalty—equally and fairly, yet the execution of the law is far from being fair and balanced. Despite the good intentions of our nation's founding fathers to "establish justice and ensure domestic tranquility,"[11] our system is corrupt because of the evil within man. It's a problem of trickle-down morality. The judges can't administer justice if their hearts don't submit to the standards of God or the mandates of Scripture. The same Ten Commandments that were sufficient to govern Israel thousands of years ago are still sufficient to govern our nation and adjudicate in our courts today.

Our law system only works when justice and righteousness prevail. Justice refers to the fairness and balance that the law grants to every one of America's citizens. Righteousness refers to the right standing that man should have with God. The irony of our justice

---

[10] Preamble to the Constitution for the United States.

[11] Preamble to the Constitution for the United States.

system's lack of success is there can be no justice without righteousness.

Righteousness also involves integrity, honesty, and truth. If the citizenry of our nation abandons right living—i.e., if the qualities of integrity, honesty, and truth are removed from society—then the common perception of what justice is will be perverted and skewed. Righteousness and justice must walk together.

Unfortunately, the sin of man compromises the practice of righteousness and justice in our legal system. The pervasiveness of sin taints and curses every aspect of life in our society. On the other hand, righteousness improves and reconciles every aspect of life in our society. That's why King Solomon asserted, "Godliness makes a nation great, but sin is a disgrace to any people" (Proverbs 14:34).

Another important aspect of the justice scales is that Lady Justice is balancing the scales blindfolded. The blindfold represents impartiality. Lady Justice cannot see the party for whom she is adjudicating a case. Therefore, she can treat every person the same. She is blind to skin color. She is impervious to prejudice. She will not yield to partiality. She will not favor one race or culture over another...or one socio-economic class over another.

Our law system works when judges, defense attorneys, and everyone in the court system practices law with impartiality. Unfortunately, plea bargain abuses in the criminal justice system violate the principle of weighing crimes and their penalties equally. The rampant misuse of plea bargaining has favored the affluent, who have the money to pay for legal teams who will acquit them even when they're guilty.

The misuse of plea bargaining racially discriminates against blacks and Latinos, as it regularly shows favoritism toward the rich and famous. Defense attorneys often rely on guilty plea bargains to lessen the sentences for uneducated, under-represented, unpolished black youths—who are innocent of wrongdoing but look too "ghetto" to be credible to a discriminating judge. As a result, the notoriety of such injustices only deepens racial wounds, and Isaiah's prophecy rings true:

"Justice is driven away, and right cannot come near. Truth stumbles in the public square, and honesty finds no place there. There is so little honesty that those who stop doing evil find themselves the victims of crime." – Isaiah 59:14–15a (GNT)

Our law system works when "mercy and truth are met together" and when "righteousness and peace have kissed each other" (Psalm 85:10). When a long-time prisoner has adequately satisfied his debt to society and consequently gets released on parole, pardoning that criminal reflects an act of mercy. However, that merciful sentence must be met with Truth. The parole or pardon is only merciful if God backs that decision or motivates that mercy sentence. If a government official extends mercy, but it's not for a godly reason, then it's not God-led mercy. It could be given to promote an agenda, to become popular with a certain constituency, or to obtain political favors in high places.

This is one of the ways corruption finds its way into the justice system. Where the sin of man compromises the practice of righteousness and justice in our legal system, it also compromises the practice of mercy and truth.

This is where the role of the church steps in! Christians, with lives reflecting the values and practices of God, should uphold and preserve the righteousness and fairness of the justice scale. Christians are the only ones in our society who operate in the invisible kingdom of heaven's Commander-in-Chief. Ultimately, the only way that America is going to achieve true justice is by obeying God and practicing the principles of the kingdom of God in our land. Then, true justice—ushered in on the shoulders of Jesus Christ—will be established in our courts. The role of the Church is crucial in eradicating the pervasive racial disparity in the criminal justice system.

Black people take to the streets whenever a police officer kills a black man but doesn't receive a life sentence or any kind of indictment. They protest because the sentencing doesn't appear to be fair. But the media is not always reporting the full story. The media doesn't reveal the background of everything that went down in order for that police shooting to take place. The reality is that the black man may have resisted arrest. So, his resistance may have started the whole conflict. Nevertheless, cries fill the streets.

Ironically, the very crowd crying out for justice is actually moving the country further away from justice. Justice requires righteousness, and you can't have justice and be crooked at the same time. You can't kill your neighbor in cold blood in your community, and then cry "murder" when a white police officer kills someone in your community.

Our Job Is to Be in Right Standing with God

Without righteousness and right standing with God, we'll never get justice. One in every sixty-five deaths of young African-American men resulted from killings by police. In fact, the rate of police-involved deaths for black men was five times higher than for white men of the same age. And yet 95% of black murders are at the hands of another black person.

Until black people are willing to deal with the fact that they're killing their own people and repent of their own wrongdoing, they're not going to witness the scales of justice tip in their favor regarding the injustices of police shootings. "Doing right brings honor to a nation, but sin brings disgrace" (Proverbs 14:34, CEV).

If we as a people are going to ask for justice, then we have to walk in justice and righteousness ourselves. Righteousness starts with a personal walk of integrity before you can ask a judge or a jury to sentence you according to righteousness and integrity.

The Ramifications That Fatherlessness Has on Race

Righteousness has the power to not only affect the justice system but also turn a whole tide of fatherless homes in the black community into strong, thriving households—thus weakening the grip of racism on our nation.

There is a strong correlation between premarital sexual activity and fatherlessness in the black community. An alarming 72 percent of black children born in America are non-marital births. This high rate of babies born in homes headed by single mothers means that today's black youth are being raised without the modeling and mentoring of a father. The consequences of today's fatherlessness far outweigh any persecution the Ku Klux Klan could have executed against the black community decades ago. Fatherlessness affects the spiritual, relational, emotional, social, economic, and academic well-being of black families.

Without a dad to set the moral standards in the home, black teenage boys wind up learning how to be a man from their peers in the streets. Thus, they are five times more likely to commit a crime. Single-parent, female-headed households are six times more likely to live in poverty—all due to the absence of a dad providing the necessary income for his family. Children raised in fatherless homes are nine times more likely to drop out of school and twenty times more likely to be incarcerated.

Monogamous Marriage and Race

Premarital sex has proven to jeopardize the likelihood of black marriages flourishing in our communities. Multiple premarital partners increase the chances of divorce—leading to the deterioration of the black family. By becoming sexually active with just one partner other than her husband, the survival rate of that woman's marriage drops from 95% to 62%. If she becomes sexually involved with two other partners, it drops to 50%.

Out of wedlock births destabilize the family unit. Sex without commitment between a man and a woman significantly reduces the chances of them ever reaching a marital commitment. Only 17 percent of black teenagers between fifteen and seventeen years of age live in a stable, two-parent home with both of their biological parents. That means 83 percent of black teens live in broken families.

In Washington, DC, only 9 percent of seventeen-year-olds live with both biological parents. In 2012, 75 percent of white two-year-old's were living with both biological parents. In comparison, only 30 percent of black two-year-old's were living with both married biological parents. That means 70 percent of young black children were living in a single-parent structure.

The long-term impact of out-of-wedlock births in the black community is multi-faceted. As a result of fatherlessness in our community, the majority of black children—especially young black males—will be predisposed to deficits in areas such as educational opportunities, income potential, personal productivity, physical and mental health, and the capacity to marry and raise their children well. Every family needs to be serving God so that a standard for living and interacting in a society is taught and upheld. There was a time in the black community when our homes were headed by a father and a mother, and both were not only attending church but also upholding the standards of the Bible. So, when things were running amuck in the black community, the parents in our community would take a stand and say, "You can act like a fool out there in the streets if you want to, but as for me and my house, we will serve the Lord!"

There was a common code of behavior that everyone in the black community believed in so that if someone was acting out in the streets, then one parent would go to the other parent and tell them what their kids were doing. There was more consistency between what we believed and how we held each other accountable to interact a certain way with each other.

Why would things be worse when we have more economic and social advancements and more freedoms than we had back then?

We walked away from God, thus we walked away from all of those principles that keep our families together. The problem with the black community is that we stopped singing "Amazing Grace," and no one ever holds others accountable in the Church.

The Paradox of the Black Church

It is vital that righteousness starts in the personal walks of every member of the black family because sin is destroying our households and communities. Black people are the most faithful demographic in America when it comes to attending church, yet black people lead in all of the demographics regarding the social ills and moral crises in

American culture. We lead in every category of death: AIDS, abortion, and homicide.

In cases where crime and murder hurt the white community, they hurt the black community far worse. According to Forbes Magazine 2016, Chicago's death toll outnumbered that of both wars in Iraq and Afghanistan combined. There were almost as many murders in that one American city between 2001 and 2016 (7,916) as there had been in the two major U.S. military wars during the same time period (6,888).

The Chicago Tribune reported that of the 592 homicides in Chicago from January 1 to October 5, 2020, 320 of the victims were African American. That's a whopping 54 percent!

We lead in case of infanticide. According to the Guttmacher Institute, in 2017, 13.5 of every 1000 women between the ages of 15 and 44 ended their pregnancies by abortion. The same institute reported that the abortion rate among African American women in the same age group was a staggering 27.1 of every 1000 women. Unfortunately, many of these women are members of a church somewhere in the black community.

Out-of-wedlock births in the black community have increased from 25 percent to 72 percent in the last fifty years. Our church-going sisters are not growing in holy living but are moving in the opposite direction with each passing decade. This disparity proves that the proclamation of Gospel truth and the demonstration of Gospel truth is not filtering through to the every-day lives of black people in America.

I say this emphatically: the black church in America has failed us as a people. The black church has not been teaching the truth. There's no preaching about sin and its repercussions. The black church has not upheld a standard of holiness. The black church has primarily been a feel-good church, where people show up and sing Gospel music and have a "Holy Ghost good time" but leave unchanged! The black church has not addressed sin and called it out for what it is before a holy God.

I can speak for myself when I confessed that as a young person, I was faithfully attending church on Sundays but getting drunk or high on Saturdays. Then I would show up in church the following morning and sit on the front pew where all the deacons sit…because I was a member of the deacon board! I was being entertained by the great music and the soul-stirring preaching, but I was returning to my lifestyle of sin throughout the week. No one confronted me about the hypocrisy of my lifestyle.

It's the 2000-pound elephant in the room. Blacks are the most church-attending ethnic group in America, yet there is a sexual and moral crisis deep in the black church, the black family, and the black community. As much as media pundits and many black leaders would like to "blame the system," this epidemic was not imposed from outside the black community but from within it.

There are several critical questions I'd like to present here:

- How do we swing the pendulum from premarital sex, divorce, abortion, cohabitation, homosexuality, and pornography addiction to restoring chastity, monogamy, and intact biblical marriages in the black community?

- Where is the message of biblical sexual purity being taught if the black church isn't addressing it?

- Why isn't the black community adhering to the actions that will strengthen the black family?

- Where is the black church in the demise of the family structure?

- How is it that the black church does not significantly benefit from monogamous marriage and does not yield the fruits of premarital abstinence and stable marriages?

- Is the black church up to the challenge to restore Christ's teaching on matters of sex and marriage?

Race and the Institution of Family

The black family is under siege more than ever. Marriage is under attack, but black marriages—due to the vulnerable areas left by the circumstances I described earlier—are most susceptible to destruction unless the Church comes to the rescue.

Marriage is a lasting covenant that should not be broken. Any sex should be within the parameters of the marriage bed. No matter how modern our practices become in American culture, God will always hate divorce. It shatters the permanent covenant that He designed for a man and woman to enjoy for a lifetime. He also knew the far-reaching ramifications of divorce on our families and our souls, and He wanted to spare us of that immense suffering and multi-generational brokenness. Jesus wants us whole. A whole family is the backbone of a thriving church, and a thriving church can then bring healing and restoration to a broken world.

The biblical standard for marriage is slowly being eradicated from our American culture. Therefore, marriage is being redefined as man's creation, not God's creation. What man creates, he can redefine. But man didn't create marriage—God did. Therefore, no one on this earth, not even in the highest court in the land, has the authority to redefine marriage. What God creates, only He can define.

Biblical marriage is between a man and a woman. It is not simply a relational preference mandated by the traditional generation. Marriage between a man and a woman originated in the mind of God.

Regrettably, our justice system has begun to break away from God's laws and God's definition of marriage. The recent Obergefell Supreme Court decision concluded that marriage was no longer just between a man and a woman but that there was a constitutional right for same-sex marriage. Thus, homosexual behavior is now a protected class just like race and gender. It bears repeating that marriage is under attack in our society and culture.

We are now living in the age of protecting transgender rights too. Even the biological sex of a man and a woman is being minimized to a subjective opinion of your sexual gender. However, Genesis 1:27–28 states this:

"So God created man in his own image, in the image of God created he him; male and female created he them. And God blessed them, and God said unto them, Be fruitful, and

multiply, and replenish the earth, and subdue it: and have dominion over the fish of the sea, and over the fowl of the air, and over every living thing that moveth upon the earth."

So many gains have been made in the devil's camp due to the Church's failure to preach the Gospel and address sin. When the Church fails to do its job, then the marriage fails. When a marriage fails, then the black family fails. When the black family fails, the community crumbles—taking with it, jobs, educational opportunities, a common standard of living, and a legacy for the next generation.

America needs to get its heart right in the area of race because when America sneezes, black America catches a cold. The black community cannot afford to persist in sexual promiscuity, drug addiction, incarceration, non-marital births, homicide, abortion, and homosexuality. Our nation's pastors and spiritual leaders must call the black community back to a biblical lifestyle of consecration and sexual purity. As the black church is healthy, America is healed.

Repentance Can Restore Justice and Restore the Brokenness in Our Communities

Ultimately, there must be repentance, revival, and reformation in the black church and subsequently the black community.

"And the LORD appeared to Solomon by night, and said unto him, I have heard thy prayer, and have chosen this place to myself for an house of sacrifice. If I shut up heaven that there be no rain, or if I command the locusts to devour the land, or if I send pestilence among my people; If my people, which are called by my name, shall humble themselves, and pray, and seek my face, and turn from their wicked ways; then will I hear from heaven, and will forgive their sin, and will heal their land. Now mine eyes shall be open, and mine ears attent unto the prayer that is made in this place." – 2 Chronicles 7:12–15

Forgiveness

I was commissioned to go to South Africa during the era of apartheid to preach forgiveness to the oppressed colored people suffering under apartheid. One of the most courageous and difficult things I've ever done was to challenge the colored people to forgive their oppressors and to wash a white South African's feet. I knew that it might come across as insensitive or offensive, but I could not fail them as an agent of reconciliation. So, I had to preach the difficult truth of the Gospel, not just give them something sweet that would tickle their ears. I had to give a radical word to remedy a radical situation.

One parishioner approached me after my message and confessed how impossible it would be to forgive his oppressors. He wanted more than anything to respond to God, but it hurt him to hear my challenge.

I told him he had to forgive his oppressors, even though they were evil, even though they were wrong for making unjust laws, even though they discriminated against him, and even though they imprisoned his people and beat them mercilessly. He was angry—and rightly so! Yet it was still God's will that he forgive these men. As long as he held on to unforgiveness, he was just as bound in sin as his oppressors were bound to racism. As long as he was bound to hatred and vengeance, he was actually in a worse state than his oppressors.

I offered to pray with him and to ask for God's empowerment to forgive them by faith. He obeyed and responded to Jesus. He was delivered from the bondage of unforgiveness and began to enjoy great peace. Years later, he contacted me and told me how much he had prospered spiritually since I brought that word. He's now a pastor of a large church, and he has asked me to come back to South Africa to speak at his conference. He calls me one of his heroes.

The truth will set people free and turn things around if the Church will be courageous enough to preach the Word in the midst of controversy—whether it's the racial conflict in America or the unjust apartheid in South Africa.

Do not be deceived. Your everyday actions have a lot to do not only with your own destiny but also with the destiny of a people. The radical solution to heal the wounds of apartheid, which I presented to believers gathered at the South African convention, is the same radical solution I admonish Americans to embrace in order to heal their racial wounds.

God cares about the racial conflict in our nation. He cares about the relational brokenness plaguing the black family. He sent His Son to die for the sins that divide the races and shatter homes. He bids the offender and offended to come and be reconciled to each other.

> *"The LORD has seen this, and he is displeased that there is no justice. He is astonished to see that there is no one to help the oppressed. So he will use his own power to rescue them and to win the victory. He will wear justice like a coat of armor and saving power like a helmet. He will clothe himself with the strong desire to set things right and to punish and avenge the wrongs that people suffer.... The LORD says to his people, 'I will come to Jerusalem to defend you and to save all of you that turn from your sins. And I make a covenant with you: I have given you my power and my teachings to be yours forever, and from now on you are to obey me and teach your children and your descendants to obey me for all time to come." (Isaiah 59:15b–17, 20–21)*

Now that our hearts have been moved by the gravity of the problem and the realization of God's desire to come to the rescue, let us discuss how we can get our hearts right in the area of race.

How to Get Your Hearts Right in the Area of Race

Have a saved and changed heart that is submitted to the Lord Jesus.
Before we can know God's heart on race, we must *have* His heart. We must come to a vertical reconciliation with God before we enter into a horizontal reconciliation with man. (See vertical reconciliation earlier in the chapter.)

Bring others to the saving knowledge of Jesus so that they have the heart to know God and understand His ways.
Once we have entered into vertical reconciliation with man, we must accept our assignment—our ministry of reconciliation—and preach Jesus to others, especially those of another race. Just as God will change our hearts in the area of

race, He will begin to change their hearts as well. All of us will come to the cross with hearts submitted and transformed by His power, growing in our knowledge of God and His ways.

Have the power to carry out His will because God has called us to be reconciled to each other.

Anything that Jesus asks us to do, He empowers us to fulfill. We need to ask Him to fill us with His Spirit. God's power is not just for "feel-good times" around the altar or during worship. His Spirit is practical and empowering. He anoints us to ensure victory and enablement for anything He wants us to pursue. As we pursue oneness and reconciliation, expect revival power to accomplish God's will.

Intervention by God.

We can't achieve racial reconciliation on our own. We are totally dependent on His power to do it. Also, we are dependent on His omniscience (His comprehensive knowledge of our spiritual state) and His omnipresence (His ability to be everywhere we are) to set the stage for His intervention.

Expect the Lord to show you areas in your heart that you weren't aware were affected by racism. Expect the Lord to push unconfessed bitterness and unforgiveness to the surface of your heart. Expect the Lord to arrange divine appointments with people with whom you need to reconcile or to whom you need to introduce His reconciling love.

Be in one accord.

Unity among the brethren invokes God's blessing and anointing. Psalm 133 (TLB) declares this:

"How wonderful it is, how pleasant, when brothers live in harmony! For harmony is as precious as the fragrant anointing oil that was poured over Aaron's head and ran down onto his beard and onto the border of his robe. Harmony is as refreshing as the dew on Mount Hermon, on

the mountains of Israel. And God has pronounced this eternal blessing on Jerusalem, even life forevermore."

When His presence infiltrates your life—whether you're pursuing reconciliation at that moment or not—your heart will become more tender to the things that are on God's heart.

a. Contrition: He will likewise bring more humility and sorrow over your sin and show you the ways that disunity and conflict have grieved His heart.

b. Holiness: The Lord will also give you a strong distaste for anything that's not representative of His character and anything that does not live in His presence—like hatred, disunity, pride, anger, vengeance, and malice. These qualities (and more) dwell at the center of racial brokenness.

1. *He will hear us and heal our land.*

As we genuinely obey God and whole-heartedly respond to His work in our lives in the area of race, our contrition and holiness will move God's heart, and He will hear us and heal the racial wounds of our land.

"If I shut up the heavens so that there is no rain, or if I command the locust to devour the land, or if I send pestilence among My people, and My people who are called by My name humble themselves and pray and seek My face and turn from their wicked ways, then I will hear from heaven, will forgive their sin and will heal their land." – 2 Chronicles 7:13–14 (NASB)

Revival

Patterns in church history show that revival always follows seasons of individual repentance, interpersonal and mass evangelism, and contrition and intercession. Expect the Lord to move in the following ways:

1. People are going to come to the Lord in droves. The church is going to catch on fire and hunger for God. The supernatural will also increase.

2. As a result, Christians are going to boldly preach Jesus and enthusiastically tell everyone about Christ. There will be a clear line drawn between good and evil. Therefore, greater judgment will come upon those who deny Christ. On one side, the fire will get hotter for the Church, and on the other side, the fire will get hotter for those who will reject Christ and refuse to follow Him.

Chapter Ten

Reconciliation or Revenge

"Every Christian is a minister of reconciliation and has the responsibility of bringing harmony where there is conflict. Put another way, Christians are God's Peace Corps." ~ Tony Evans[12]

"With his own body he broke down the wall that separated them and kept them enemies." – Ephesians 2:14b (GNT)

America's Issue of Race

As I mentioned in the earlier chapter, I grew up in Atlanta, Georgia, during the politically and socially volatile 1960s and '70s. As a child, I remember when Martin Luther King was killed, and I watched his funeral procession through the streets of downtown Atlanta. I remember the race riots that erupted all over the country as a result of Dr. King's assassination.

Many social and political advances have been made since then, but one thing remains the same: the country I live in now is as racially charged as the country I grew up in. Despite the social improvements and legal changes to Jim Crow laws, there is a greater change that must take place in the hearts of every successive generation in America. And if that foundational change does not take place, the same issues will follow us into the next decades of America's history. The hearts and minds of Americans have to be renewed in the area of race.

---

[12] Tony Evans, *Tony Evans' Book of Illustrations: Stories, Quotes, and Anecdotes from More Than 30 years of Preaching and Public Speaking* (Chicago, IL: Moody Publishers, 2009), 243.

As Christians, our minds are not renewed overnight. We still bring garbage from our former lives to the other side of the cross! God had to deal with me. It was a process. When I was filled with the Holy Spirit, I began to hunger for God. My spiritual hunger and thirst for God was so great that it took me past my ethnic comfort zone making me willing to learn from other people outside my culture.

If you are totally yielded to God, you shouldn't put up a wall when God wants to bring His TRUTH to you through anyone regardless of culture or race that's not your own.

Racial Identity? Or Identity in Christ?

God wants our self-image to be rooted in our spiritual reality first. Then this vantage point—being seated with Christ in heavenly places (Ephesians 2:6)—will "color" everything we approach in life…even race relations.

Wellington Boone, the author of *Breaking Through*, noted this:

> *"Our problem in this nation is not a skin problem, but a sin problem. We have gained the potential for reconciliation by the blood of Christ but haven't practiced reconciling our hearts to each other. We may have come over on different boats, but we are in the same boat now and it is adrift on a sea of hate."[13]*

In the name of racial solidarity, black Christians have adopted a race-based or race-centered mindset and have swapped sound biblical theology for a spiritual perspective that is highly influenced by Black Nationalist thought. In many cases, remnants of the Nation of Islam ideology have crept into the black church. However, I take the same position as Boone in this regard: "Louis Farrakhan and the Nation of Islam are diametrically opposed to Christianity."[14]

---

[13] Wellington Boone, Breaking Through…p. 85
[14] Wellington Boone, Breaking Through…p. 84

Elijah Muhammad says of Christianity:

"It is a religion organized and backed by the white devils for the purpose of making slaves of black mankind."

"[Allah] said that Christianity was organized by the white race and they placed the name of Jesus on it as being the founder and author to deceive black people into accepting it."

"Once the so-called Negroes drop the religion of slavery (Christianity) and accept Allah for their God and his religion (Islam), Allah will remove their fear and grief, and they will not fear and grieve anymore."

"[Jesus] was only a prophet like Moses and the other prophets and had the same religion (Islam). He did his work and is dead like others of his time, and has not knowledge of their prayers to him."

"It is far more important to teach separation of the blacks and whites in America than prayer. Teach and train the blacks to do something for self in the way of uniting and seeking a home on this earth that they can call their own. There is no such thing as living in peace with white Americans."

"They are opposed to reconciliation among blacks and whites and even hold to the bizarre belief that white people are devils created by an evil scientist named Yacub."

"Such marches led by Farrakhan have been condemned openly as well as endorsed, but the questions from my heart that I have to ask of the Christians who supported him are: Is there any limitation or qualification that you will set regarding a person's beliefs or lifestyle that would prohibit you from following him? Is there anything that will offend your Christian faith enough to force you to forsake black unity? By supporting this march, many proved that their answer to both of these questions is a hearty no."[15]

---

[15] Wellington Boone, Breaking Through…p. 84–85.

As Christians who have become new creations in Christ—having left behind the old and embraced the new—we must leave behind any vestiges of theology that contradict the teachings of Scripture and prevent us from uniting with our white brothers and sisters in Christ.

The "Get It Syndrome"

Within the body of Christ, we're in a "get it syndrome." When I talk to black people, they say, "White folks don't get it. Nor do they want to get it. They don't know our history. They don't know our culture. They don't understand how the impact of slavery and the cruel, involuntary separation of our families have destroyed our ancestry. They don't understand the effect that Jim Crow laws had on our social, political, and financial well-being."

When I talk to white people, they say, "I get it. Now, black folks need to get *over* it! Racism no longer exists. You had a black president in the White House! You no longer need any special treatment or consideration. Besides, we didn't do anything to you. It was our forefathers who made all of the mistakes, not us. So, get over it!"

Consequently, an invisible gulf exists between the races because of the "get it" syndrome. This gulf represents misunderstandings by both parties. In order to bridge that gulf, members of both races must listen with spiritual ears to truly empathize with each other.

Black Lives Matter

The Black Lives Matter Movement brings a similar controversy. In response to the police shootings of unarmed black men, the Black Lives Matter Movement was created to help law enforcement "get it"—to think twice before you shoot a black person because his or her life is just as important as a white person's life.

The response to the chant that black lives matter is "Of course, black lives matter. In fact, all lives matter!" Consequently, after numerous retaliatory killings were levied against police officers, the law enforcement community began to promote, "Blue lives matter."

My warning to all of the parties represented on either side of the controversy is this: do not retaliate in anger when you disagree with an act of alleged injustice because you will bring a curse upon yourself. Any act of vengeance in which innocent lives are taken is a serious offense before God. He will visit those who take innocent blood because innocent blood will begin to cry out from the ground. Retaliation is not the answer to injustice.

The Black Lives Matter Movement is not the best solution to racial inequality and prejudice in America for several reasons. First, the movement doesn't have a moral foundation. According to their website, it was started by three lesbian women who are promoting civil rights not only for African Americans but also for homosexuals, transexuals, and those committed to deviant behavior and lifestyles. They represent and endorse many forms of ungodliness.

Secondly, Black Lives Matter has broadened its purpose beyond racial inequality and prejudice. They've become advocates for slavery reparations and a host of other nationalistic causes that "push the envelope" in extremity. Their platform also has a socialist focus.

Thirdly, the Movement lacks a cohesive operation. It's loosely organized, and outside groups have already begun to take advantage of its purpose. Because its focus is so splintered, its effectiveness against even the decent causes could prove to be minimal over time.

The Validity of the Black Lives Controversy

While the Black Lives Matter Movement has skewed solutions and approaches to the racial disparity and demise of the black community, the problem is valid. Many of the stark statistics concerning the black community are born out of racial brokenness. An African-American minister once shared this allegory with his congregation.

> *"A man visited the doctor one day as he was in excruciating pain. The doctor asked him where it hurt and the man told him 'all over.' There was not a part of the man that was not hurting. The doctor told him to touch his shoulder. The man did and immediately hollered. The doctor told him to touch his own thigh. The man screamed. The doctor told him to touch his forehead. The man did and then yelled in agony. The doctor said, 'I've never seen anything like this in my life.*

Let's try one more thing…touch your toes.' The patient touched his toes and grimaced. 'Oh Doc, everywhere I touch I hurt.' The doctor examined him and said, 'No wonder, you've got a dislocated finger!'"
"Many of us have experienced this phenomenon where everywhere we turn in life seems to be painful but only due to one specific area of hurt that is radiating into every other area of our lives."[16]

When America sneezes, "Black America" catches a cold. All of the mitigating factors that cause the average white American a temporary setback in life, unfortunately, tend to cause permanent damage to black Americans.

In cases where crime and murder hurt the white community, they hurt the black community far worse! Young black men were nine times more likely than other Americans to be killed by police officers in 2015, according to the findings of a Guardian study that recorded a final tally of 1,134 deaths at the hands of law enforcement officers that year.

Despite the fact that they make up only two percent of the total U.S. population, African-American males between the ages of fifteen and thirty-four comprised more than 15 percent of all deaths logged in 2016 by an ongoing investigation into the use of deadly force by police. Paired with official government mortality data, this new finding indicates that about one in every sixty-five deaths of a young African-American man in the U.S. is a killing by police. Their rate of police-involved deaths was five times higher than that of white men the same age.

The number one cause of death among young men between the ages of fifteen and thirty-four is murder. Sadly, ninety-five percent of those murdered were killed at the hands of a fellow black man. So, the overwhelming majority of male murders in the black community are murders committed against each other. Do those black lives matter

---

[16] Tony Evans, *Tony Evans' Book of Illustrations: Stories, Quotes, and Anecdotes from More Than 30 years of Preaching and Public Speaking* (Chicago, IL: Moody Publishers, 2009), 216.

to the black men who extinguished them? Or do black lives only matter if they're killed by a white person?

The death rate among the unborn in the black community is just as staggering. Black people comprise only 13 percent of the population in America, yet 40 percent of the abortions that take place in America are performed on black women.

Seventy percent of all black families are headed by a single woman—with no father in the home. It is a sobering reality that 7 out of 10 black youths are growing up without both parents to guide and nurture them. This is especially significant for boys because while girls may still have a mother to model life for them, boys need a father—the main man God designated to mentor and teach them in life.

Without a father in the home, who teaches them about life? They learn about life out in the streets! What life lessons are the streets teaching them? The streets are teaching them to rebel. So, when a police officer shows up on the scene, the young men are taught not to comply. They're encouraged to rebel against the police and those in authority to show their manhood. This kind of misguided bravado has gotten many black teens shot and killed unnecessarily.

One aspect of the fearless, tough-guy bravado is conveying that you're not afraid to go to prison. Incarceration becomes a community culture. In fact, prison becomes a badge of honor because a prison bit proves that you know how to survive no matter what downturns happen in life.

America mourned when Philando Castille was shot and killed in Minnesota. His girlfriend had been beside him, videotaping the whole incident on Facebook Live. Like a surreal drama, she described the fatality as it was unfolding: a gun pointing through the car window, Philando had been shot and was dying in the seat beside her.

In the case of Alton Sterling in Baton Rouge, Louisiana, America mourned as we watched Alton down on the ground, and the police officer shooting him in the chest. It was all videotaped.

Other horrific deaths by police shootings include Michael Brown—shot and killed in Ferguson, Missouri; Freddie Gray shot and killed in Baltimore, Maryland; and twelve-year-old Tamir Rice shot and killed in Cleveland, Ohio. Eric Garner died because of an illegal chokehold by New York City Police. Most recently, George Floyd in Minneapolis, Minnesota, died after a white police officer knelt on his neck for eight minutes and forty-six seconds until his breath was gone.

The video of George Floyd's death circulated through news and social media outlets worldwide, sparking outrage among blacks everywhere and opening the eyes of non-blacks to the racial injustices that blacks have decried for decades. Peaceful protests, violent riots, and prayer vigils have been held in every major US city and various smaller towns. Citizens are calling on their government representatives for reform in police departments and the criminal justice system. Employees are demanding that corporate leaders acknowledge racial inequities and take a public stand to work toward equality.

The grief from these lost lives is resonating around the country. The Black Lives Matter Movement was a reflex-expression of deep sorrow and anguish reacting to continuous murders within our borders. These sudden deaths created a permanent disturbance of kinship. Families lost brothers, fathers, nephews, and sons. Communities lost coworkers and neighbors. Whether the murders occurred justifiably or not, their losses among black families in this country should cause us to mourn as a nation.

Additionally, we must evaluate these events in light of a bigger picture: the cumulative effect of a four-hundred-year history of slavery, then systemic racism, then unjust treatment during the Jim Crow era in which government abusers were spared from indictment, and then police brutality during the peaceful demonstrations of the Civil Rights movement that was never punished. The conflicts erupting now may seem like over-reactions and exaggerations, but the police brutality and homicides of the past three years have served as a toothpick proverbially breaking the camel's back.

Like steam bursting from a faulty water heater, past racial injustices have elevated the pressure of current crises. Meanwhile, the communities who haven't experienced the same severity of conditions wonder why the explosive combustion. Sometimes, things get stored up because of history.

In streets throughout our country, people are slaying one another because they don't value life. If you don't have an appreciation for God as the Giver of life, you won't respect other people's lives.

What must you do if you have been sinned against in the area of racial discrimination or racial injustice?

Both the Oppressed and Oppressor Need Comfort

The members of the Black Lives Matter Movement are asking for the world to sympathize with the injustices of police brutality victims. The police response that "Blue Lives Matter" maintains that anarchy and disrespect cannot be tolerated in our country. Both sides are mourning losses. Both sides need to be comforted.

> *"So I returned, and considered all the oppressions that are done under the sun: and behold the tears of such as were oppressed, and they had no comforter; and on the side of their oppressors there was power; but they had no comforter." – Ecclesiastes 4:1*

Jesus Interceded on Behalf of His Disciples

Relational harmony is near and dear to Jesus' heart. It's what He died to offer us—a harmony with Him that we could not achieve apart from His forgiveness and blood sacrifice.

> *"I am praying not only for these disciples but also for all who will ever believe in me through their message. I pray that they will all be one, just as you and I are one—as you are in me, Father, and I am in you. And may they be in us so that the world will believe you sent me."*
>
> *"I have given them the glory you gave me, so they may be one as we are one. I am in them and you are in me. May they experience such perfect unity that the world will know that you sent me and that you love them as much as you love me." – John 17:20–23 (NLT)*

If you suspect that a racial offense could be standing between you and a brother or sister in Christ, "bust a move," as the younger generation might say. Take the initiative to seek reconciliation.

> *"Therefore if thou bring thy gift to the altar, and there rememberest that thy brother hath ought against thee; Leave there thy gift before the altar, and go thy way; first be reconciled to thy brother, and then come and offer thy gift."*
> *– Matthew 5:23–24*

Practical Steps

We've explored the ills in the black community in America and the ways in which those ills ignite and exacerbate racial tensions in the U.S.

Now, what role does the Church play in the healing of America? What will Christians need to do to bring unity to the racial division and social unrest we're witnessing? How can racial harmony become a commonly experienced reality in our country and not just an ascribed ideal?

- Black and white leaders and all Christians must work to have genuine relationships. Listen to each other. Love each other.

- Black and white pastors, leaders, and congregations must pray together and cry out for revival, the outpouring of the Holy Spirit, and God's mercy and forgiveness.

  Black and white pastors and congregations must work together to further the great commission.

- White Christians must join the leadership of black Christian leaders to show their willingness to humble themselves to black leadership.

- The white Church must dedicate resources to partner with ministries to accomplish the mission of reaching young black adults.

- The Church must demonstrate oneness to the world at every opportunity to glorify Jesus Christ.

The interdependence and cooperation of the black church and the white church can demonstrate a racial harmony that this watching world could only dream of. The power of love and unity will break the back of the segregation, hatred, and racism in our nation.

The Upper Room Experience

"And when the day of Pentecost was fully come, they were all with one accord in one place." – Acts 2:1

There is much that modern-day Christians can learn from the experience of the early church in that Upper Room. Luke recorded that "they were all with one accord in one place." They didn't habitually gather together there because they were "devout pilgrims from all over the world" (Acts 2:5 MSG).

The believers had to stay in the Upper Room and pray until they were in one accord. About 120 people were gathered there when the Holy Spirit's presence and power visited them.

What we can learn from this text is that the Church isn't going to achieve unity simply by gathering together and singing "Kumbaya." Christians—just like the early Church—will have to labor in prayer together to see a mighty move of God's Spirit, who brings true "heart unity."

"And suddenly there came a sound from heaven as of a rushing mighty wind, and it filled all the house where they were sitting. And there appeared unto them cloven tongues like as of fire, and it sat upon each of them. And they were all filled with the Holy Ghost, and began to speak with other tongues, as the Spirit gave them utterance. And there were dwelling at Jerusalem Jews, devout men, out of every nation under heaven. Now when this was noised abroad, the multitude came together, and were confounded, because that

every man heard them speak in his own language." – Acts 2:2–6

Gathered in that Upper Room were Jews of deep faith from *every nation of the world*. God sovereignly and intentionally assembled a variety of believers for this special time in Church history. He is the Creator of diversity. On the day of Pentecost, He not only wanted to make sure that they demonstrated unity but reflected multiplicity. Because those gathered in that room were from *"every nation under heaven"* (Acts 2:5b), the crowd who heard them could bear witness to this supernatural demonstration because they heard them speaking in the multiplicity of languages from other parts of the world. Luke describes that a crowd quickly collected and were bewildered by it.

God could have chosen to spread the news about His long-awaited impartation any way He wanted. He elected this setting of diverse nations so that witnesses could see the power of the Holy Ghost coming and hear these men speaking in their own languages.

It reminds me of how news travels instantaneously around the world nowadays via the Internet. An event taking place in China or Europe can cross the world, through the Internet, within minutes. Things can go viral within twenty-four hours. Imagine if a revival broke out in America, and then news of that revival traveled to another continent within the same day!

Although these "Upper Room believers" didn't have the technology of the Internet, the Holy Ghost's visitation was still able to reach the world because the nations were present to witness and experience that special moment. The Lord had convened His own version of a United Nations summit for the purpose of glorifying and spreading His prophetic voice in the earth. God's first-century "instant-messaging" was unfolding as these onlookers were listening to the voice of the Spirit and divine utterances.

The voice of God is not limited by culture. When God is ready to speak to someone, He can supersede language barriers, cultural differences, and regional distances to get His message to someone. Such was the case with the Upper Room experience.

"And they were all amazed and marvelled, saying one to another, Behold, are not all these which speak Galilaeans? And how hear we every man in our own tongue, wherein we were born? Parthians, and Medes, and Elamites, and the dwellers in Mesopotamia, and in Judaea, and Cappadocia, in Pontus, and Asia, Phrygia, and Pamphylia, in Egypt, and in the parts of Libya about Cyrene, and strangers of Rome, Jews and proselytes, Cretes and Arabians, we do hear them speak in our tongues the wonderful works of God. And they were all amazed, and were in doubt, saying one to another, What meaneth this?" – Acts 2:7–12

In our times, another great move of God's Spirit will occur—another Great Awakening. When God begins to manifest His presence in ways and levels that the Church has not experienced Him, every nation and every culture will hear His voice in their own tongue.

The Azusa Street Revival

"The color line was washed away in the Blood." – Frank Bartleman

A 20th-century example of an outpouring of God's Spirit that unified different races and cultures is the Azusa Street revival. This spiritual awakening in American church history was named after the Apostolic Faith Mission's address—302 Azusa Street—where Los Angeles-area believers gathered in 1906, and the power of the Holy Spirit fell upon them. The sustained presence of God, accompanied by conversions, healings, speaking in tongues, and miracles, laid the foundation for the expression of the modern-day Pentecostal movement.

As pastor of the Apostolic Faith Mission, where the historic revival broke out, William Seymour is a symbol of the racial unity among Christians that resulted from this move of God. As a black man who grew up in the segregated South and whose parents were former slaves, Seymour encountered much racism. He was a Holiness minister who was intrigued by the outpouring of the Holy Spirit taking place at a Bible college in Houston, Texas.

His desire to experience more of God's power and presence led him to attend a class led by Charles Parham, a white pastor and founder of the Apostolic Faith Movement. Due to Jim Crow laws that were in effect during the turn of the century, Seymour was not allowed to sit in the classroom with white people. Perched in the hallway, Seymour listened to Parham's teachings about the Holy Spirit.[17] This speaks of his hunger for more of God no matter the boundaries and obstacles.

Even though Seymour had not yet had the Pentecostal experience of speaking in tongues, he was so zealous about Parham's messages that he began to teach them as well. Seymour would teach segregated black audiences about the baptism of the Holy Spirit, and Parham would address segregated white audiences.

The miracle of unifying the races happened when Seymour moved to Los Angeles and was baptized with the Holy Spirit. Due to the move of God and a spiritual hunger among Christians in that area, he held standing-room-only prayer meetings in a humble storage building that both whites and blacks attended. People showed up in droves to experience God's unprecedented presence there. The fame of the Azusa Street revival quickly spread as hundreds of Christians filled the building to encounter the outpouring of God's Spirit. William Seymour had begun not only to pioneer a Pentecostal revival but also interracial worship services during a season of racial division and hostility.

Frank Bartleman, an itinerant evangelist and journalist who wrote eyewitness accounts of the Azusa Street revival, left one of Seymour's worship services, reporting, "The color line was washed away in the Blood."[18]

---

[17] *William J. Seymour Biography – Azusa Street,*
http://azusastreet.org/WilliamJSeymour.htm.

[18] Bartleman's How Pentecost Came to Los Angeles, Vinson Synan, ed. Azusa Street (Plainfield, nj: Bridge Publishing, 1980), IX–XXV.

Dr. Vincent Synan, who authored numerous publications on the Pentecostal and charismatic movement, wrote:

"The most striking and unusual feature of the Azusa Street meeting was the racial harmony that prevailed under the leadership of Seymour...Many people were amazed. In the most racist period of American history, thousands of whites came to Azusa Street and submitted to church leadership that in the beginning was essentially African American. Although whites soon became the majority, Seymour continued as pastor and exercised pastoral and spiritual authority over the meetings. As African-American hands were laid on the heads of white seekers, they were baptized in the Holy Spirit. They also looked to Seymour as their teacher and spiritual father."[19]

Because of Seymour's humility (despite racial injustice) and his persistence and steadfastness in prayer, God could use him to usher in a spiritual revival and racial integration.

Unfortunately, more than a century after the Azusa Street revival, the most segregated hour in America is Sunday morning—when Christians attend their local church. When you do find a racially diverse church, the senior pastor is typically white—not African American as Seymour was. But this next move of the Spirit is going to not only erase color lines in the Church once again but also mix up the leadership of our churches. The Holy Spirit is not bound by culture and race.

"Although the Movement began among whites in Topeka under Parham," Dr. Vinson noted, "many historians now believe the Movement became a worldwide phenomenon with the African Americans at Azusa Street. African-American worship styles spread worldwide from Azusa Street."[20]

---

[19] "The Lasting Legacies of the Azusa Street Revival," Synan, Vinson. http://enrichmentjournal.ag.org/200602/200602_142_Legacies.cfm.

[20] "The Lasting Legacies of the Azusa Street Revival," Synan, Vinson. http://enrichmentjournal.ag.org/200602/200602_142_Legacies.cfm.

Dr. Vinson also added that many well-known Pentecostal denominations have roots in Azusa Street.

> *"The Movement spread around the world under the exciting ministries of the Azusa Street Pilgrims who received their Pentecostal experiences at Azusa Street....The first Pentecostal denominations were located in the American South where Pentecostalism initially gained a mass grassroots following. Most of these denominations had been formed before 1900. They were made up of churches that added the Pentecostal experience as a third blessing—an addition to salvation and entire sanctification. These included: the Church of God in Christ (Memphis, Tennessee), the Pentecostal Holiness Church (North Carolina), The Church of God (Cleveland, Tennessee), the United Holy Church (North Carolina), and the Pentecostal Free Will Baptist Church (North Carolina).... Every classical Pentecostal movement around the world can trace its spiritual roots, directly or indirectly, to the humble mission on Azusa Street."*[21]

When God begins to break out, color won't matter! There's going to be a move of the Holy Spirit for those who have freedom of heart. The outpouring that took place in the book of Acts will once again manifest among believers of all nationalities and races today. Christians who are not bound by culture or race and are willing to yield to God's Spirit will be baptized in the Holy Ghost and prophesy and preach the gospel on the streets. White Christians are going to cross color lines to witness to blacks, and black Christians are going to cross color lines to witness to whites.

The Apostle Peter and the Apostle Paul were surprised when God called them to preach the gospel to Gentiles and not just the Jews. Likewise, the cultures that are the most foreign to you now, you may

---

[21] "The Lasting Legacies of the Azusa Street Revival," Synan, Vinson. http://enrichmentjournal.ag.org/200602/200602_142_Legacies.cfm.

be called to reach. Many of those foreigners live in your hometown. You won't have to travel across the world to reach them!

God's unifying work through the outpouring of the Holy Spirit is the answer to today's racial divisions and conflicts. A watching world witnessed Jews from different nations unify under the blanket of God's anointing. During the era of segregation in our country, a watching world witnessed blacks and whites unify under the blanket of God's anointing. We must make Americans exclaim once again, "The color line was washed away in the Blood!"

"There is no longer Jew or Gentile, slave or free, male and female. For you are all one in Christ Jesus." – Galatians 3:28 (NLT)

About the Author

Garland R. Hunt, is a proven strategic leader with a dynamic ministry background and extensive experience in advocacy for religious freedom, racial reconciliation, and criminal justice reform.

After completing a B.A. from Howard University in 1980 and JD from Howard University School of Law in 1983, he served as a judicial law clerk and staff attorney with the US Court of Appeals for the Fourth Circuit. In 1993, he founded the Raleigh International Church, an influential ministry with the mission of reconciliation in Raleigh, NC. Hunt also co-founded a strong multiracial group of over one hundred Raleigh pastors called Pastors for Awakening and Reconciliation (PAR). Hunt moved from Raleigh, NC in 1999 to his hometown of Atlanta, GA to serve as executive pastor of The Father's House. He also acted as chief operating officer of the church, while providing leadership development and training to staff and volunteers.

His senior executive leadership spans over thirty-five years, with the Fellowship of International Churches, Wellington Boone Ministries, and New Generation Campus Ministries. He has served in board leadership roles with the Association of Paroling Authorities International (APAI) and Crossroads Prison Ministries. In 2004, he was appointed to the Georgia State Board of Pardons and Paroles by Governor Sonny Perdue and served as chairman of the parole board in 2006-2008. In 2010, Hunt was appointed commissioner of the Georgia Department of Juvenile Justice. In 2011-2013, he served as president of Prison Fellowship, the world's largest prison ministry, founded by Chuck Colson. Since 2015, Hunt has served as senior pastor of The Father's House in the Atlanta, GA area. In 2018, he co-founded OneRace, a movement to promote racial reconciliation and healing within the church through prayer, fasting and genuine relationships across Atlanta, and the Southeast. OneRace has hosted reconciliation events with over twenty thousand participants praying for revival and oneness in the body of Christ.

https://www.facebook.com/profile.php?id=100000469287248
https://www.facebook.com/garlandrhunt